Equity in Your Coaching

First published 2001

sports coach UK is the brand name of The National Coaching Foundation and has been such since April 2001.

ISBN-13: 978-1-902523-41-5
ISBN-10: 1-902523-41-5

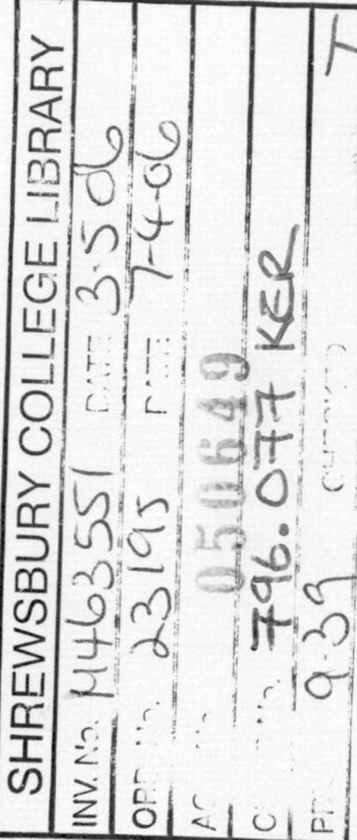

sports coach UK
114 Cardigan Road, Headingley, Leeds, LS6 3BJ
Tel: 0113-274 4802 Fax: 0113-275 5019
Email: coaching@sportscoachuk.org
Website: www.sportscoachuk.org

Author
Annie Kerr

Editor
Nicola Cooke

Sub-editors
Michelle Vernon-Way, Warwick Andrews

Typesetter
Natalie Schmidt

Cover photos
All photos courtesy of **sports coach UK**

The publishers would like to thank the following for their valuable input to this handbook:
Cathy Hughes (Women's Sports Foundation)
Mahesh Patel (English Federation of Disability Sport)
Novlette Rennie (Sporting Equals)
Sport England
sportscotland
Sports Council for Northern Ireland
Sports Council for Wales
UK Sport

Published on behalf of **sports coach UK** by
Coachwise Business Solutions
Chelsea Close
Off Amberley Road
Armley
Leeds LS12 4HP
Tel: 0113-231 1310 Fax: 0113-231 9606
Email: enquiries@coachwise.ltd.uk Website: www.1st4sport.com

Ref: 050007

Preface

Think back to the first time you took part in your sport. Imagine if your coach had told you you couldn't participate because you had a disability. What if your coach had insisted you wear specific sports clothing, but for religious reasons you couldn't and therefore wouldn't have been able to take part. How would this have made you feel? It's certainly unlikely you would have been able to progress to the stage you're at in your sport today.

Coaching is first and foremost about people – encouraging them to enjoy the positive benefits of sport and helping them achieve their potential. Everyone should have access to sport, regardless of gender, age, race, ability, faith or sexual orientation. Although we may like to think this is the case, in reality it is not. Research has shown that many groups of people are under-represented in all areas of sport, including coaching. For example, from the Moscow Olympics in 1980 to the Sydney Olympics in 2000, the number of female coaches within the British team fell from 9% to 7.6%, despite the rise in the number of female athletes competing.

Everyone involved in sport has a responsibility to improve this situation – as a coach, you have an important role to play. Sports equity and being equitable means ensuring your coaching sessions are fair, open and accessible to everyone who wants to take part. This might seem a daunting prospect, but don't worry. It doesn't mean having to learn a whole new set of coaching skills, it's more about applying and extending your existing skills and experience to meet the needs of present and potential participants. *Equity in Your Coaching* will help you do this.

Although many different groups of people are disadvantaged in sport, this pack will focus on three groups that generally experience discrimination on a more regular basis, not only in sport, but in their daily lives in general:

- Disabled people
- People from ethnic minorities
- Women and girls.

These are referred to as key target groups.

The aim is not to judge or criticise your coaching practice or opinions, but to raise your awareness of equity issues and help you identify ways of becoming a more equitable coach. By adopting the principles highlighted in this pack, you will help make your sport enjoyable and accessible to all sections of society, and hopefully attract new participants to your coaching sessions.

Each section of the pack provides information, activities and questions to help you check your own understanding and apply it to your own coaching. By the end of the pack, you should be able to:

- explain what sports equity means and why it is important
- identify barriers that may prevent the key target groups from participating in sport
- be aware of the appropriate language and terminology to use when referring to the key target groups
- overcome the barriers that may prevent the key target groups from participating in sport
- challenge inequitable behaviour during your coaching sessions
- interpret the legal framework that affects coaching
- develop an equity action plan
- know who to contact for additional information relating to coaching the key target groups.

The pack supports a three-hour **sports coach UK** workshop, which you are strongly recommended to attend. This will help you put the theory behind equity into practice and apply it to your own coaching. All coaches are offered access to support and advice after the workshop. Workshop dates and locations are available from your Regional Training Unit (see page 111 of this pack for contact details).

Key to symbols used in the text			
	Activity.		Points of interest.
	Stop and consider.		Remember.
	Important information.		Refer to the appropriate page or section specified in the resource for more information.

Contents

Appendices 119

sports coach UK

Section One

Setting the Context

1.0 What's In It For You?

The aim of this pack is to help you apply and extend your existing skills and experience to make your coaching sessions accessible to all members of the community. Before exploring exactly how to do this, it is important that you understand the concept of sports equity and why it is so important. This may seem a daunting prospect, especially if the subject is completely new to you. However, this section will provide you with useful background information and help you understand that sports equity is not simply about making sport more *politically correct*, but about improving sporting opportunities for everyone.

By the end of the section, you should be able to explain:

- what sports equity means
- which groups of people are regularly disadvantaged in sport
- why sports equity is important.

1.1 What is Sports Equity?

> *Sports equity is about fairness in sport, equality of access, recognising inequalities and taking steps to address them. It is about changing the culture and structure of sport to ensure that it becomes equally accessible to everyone in society.*
>
> *Sport England, 2000*[1]

Achieving sports equity depends on everybody involved in sport:

- recognising that certain groups of people are disadvantaged[2] and may therefore be discriminated[3] against because of their gender, age, race, ability, faith or sexual orientation, not just in sport, but in society in general
- treating everyone equally, but recognising that some groups of people have different needs
- sharing resources and making sport accessible to disadvantaged groups of people.

1.2 Who is Disadvantaged in Sport?

Everyone is treated unfairly in some way at times – no doubt you can think of a few occasions when you've been on the receiving end of unfair treatment. The following activity asks you to think of an example from your own experiences.

ACTIVITY 1

Think of an incident, not necessarily in sport, when you felt you were treated unfairly. Make a brief note of the incident in the spaces provided below and answer the questions that follow on page 3.

1 Sport England (2000) *Making English sport inclusive: equity guidelines for governing bodies.* London, Sport England. Ref no: SE/1043/1M/6/00

2 and 3 For a definition of this and other terms associated with sports equity, see Appendix A.

Why do you think you were treated unfairly?

How did this make you feel?

What effect did it have on you?

What did you do about it?

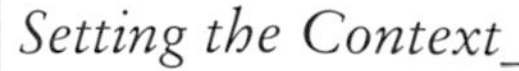

Now compare your experience with those described in the following scenarios:

Scenario 1

Tariq is a wheelchair user and a coach at a local table tennis club. The club has had a very successful season and is in a good position to win the league, with Tariq being an important member of the coaching team. The head coach wants to move the training session to what he feels is a better venue nearer to where he lives. However, this venue is not accessible to wheelchairs – there are no parking facilities, there are steps up to the main entrance but no ramp and the changing rooms are very small and cramped.

Scenario 2

Palvinda is Asian and has been a member of her local netball club for some time. She has recently been selected for the club team and will be competing regularly in local and regional tournaments. Her coach insists that all team members wear the official team kit during team training sessions and at all competitions. However, this includes a sports skirt, which Palvinda cannot wear for religious reasons – she usually wears tracksuit bottoms instead.

Scenario 3

Jackie is an avid squash player and has been top of the women's squash ladder at her local club for several months. To make things more challenging and improve her game further, she asks if she can join the men's squash ladder instead. However, the club chair says that this is against club regulations and that the men wouldn't think she was good enough to play against them.

Tariq, Palvinda and Jackie all have something in common – they've all been treated unfairly in their sport:

- Tariq feels that, by suggesting the club venue is moved, the head coach is acting unfairly. Although probably not intending to discriminate against Tariq, he has failed to realise how difficult it will make things for him. It'll be harder for Tariq to get to the venue and, once he's there, it'll be difficult for him to get into the building itself, as well as make use of the changing facilities.
- Palvinda feels that her coach is acting unreasonably when she insists that Palvinda wear a sports skirt, particularly as wearing tracksuit bottoms instead would pose no threat to her safety.
- Jackie feels she is being discriminated against because she is a woman. She is annoyed that the club chair assumes the men will think she's not good enough to play against them and that he refuses to consider reviewing club regulations or giving her the opportunity to prove her ability.

Although many different groups of people are disadvantaged in sport, Tariq, Palvinda and Jackie each belong to particular groups of people who generally experience discrimination on a more regular basis, not only in sport, but in their daily lives in general:

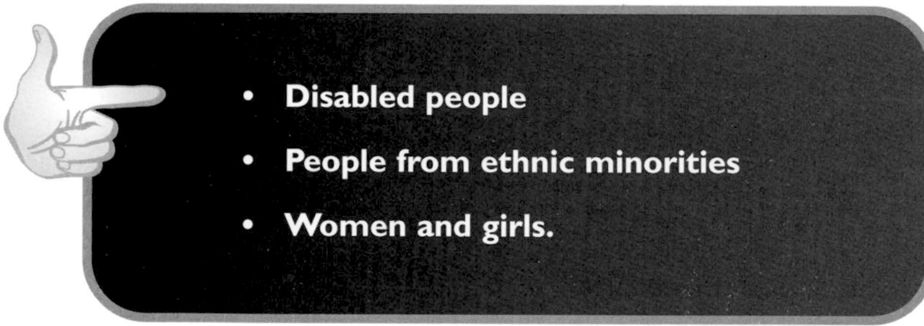

- **Disabled people**
- **People from ethnic minorities**
- **Women and girls.**

This pack will focus on these three groups. From now on, the term *key target groups* will be used when referring to them collectively.

Remember!

- For ease of reference, the guidance in this pack is often divided into separate sections for each of the three key target groups. However, this doesn't mean that each group should be treated in isolation from the other two. Remember, some of the people you coach may belong to a combination of groups (eg Asian women, disabled participants from ethnic minorities), so it's important to understand the needs of **all** the key target groups.
- Although this pack concentrates on three key target groups, remember that these aren't the only ones and that other groups of people may be disadvantaged in your sport. It's important to identify who these people are and to seek specific advice from appropriate sources.

Action Plus

1.3 Why is Sports Equity Important?

Think back to the main elements of the definition of sports equity introduced on page 2:

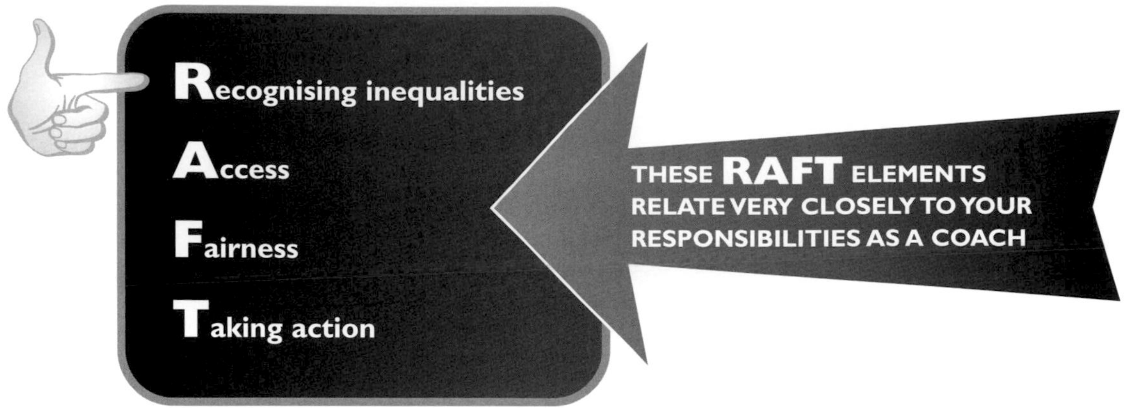

Recognising Inequalities

Society should be reflected in sport. For example, the 2001 Census revealed that the national population included:

- 55% women
- 5% disabled people
- 10% people from ethnic minorities.

However, a survey[1] carried out by the Office of National Statistics on behalf of Sport England revealed that the overall participation rate for:

- ethnic minority groups is 40% compared with a national average of 46%
- men from ethnic minorities is 49% compared with a national average of 54%
- women from ethnic minorities is 32% compared with a national average of 39%.

The findings from the research also concluded that the picture is much more complex than simply looking at participation rates, as there is considerable variation in the levels of participation between:

- different ethnic groups
- men and women
- different sports.

For example, on average, the participation rates for Black Caribbean (39%), Indian (39%) and, in particular, Pakistani (31%) and Bangladeshi (30%) populations are below the national average (46%). Only the participation rate for the Black Other group (60%) is higher than the national average.

1 Rowe, N and Champion, R (2000) *Sports participation and ethnicity in England: national survey 1999/2000 headline findings*. London, Sport England. SE/1073

It also recognised that in some sports, participation rates for ethnic minority groups are relatively high. Some examples are provided in Tables 1 and 2 below.

Table 1: Sports participation rates among men from ethnic minority groups

Sport	Participation Rate of Ethnic Minority Groups	National Average Participation Rate
Basketball	Black Caribbean (4%) Black African (4%)	1%
Badminton	Chinese (17%)	3%
Cricket	Pakistani (10%) Black Other (8%) Indian (6%)	2%

Table 2: Sports participation rates among women from ethnic minority groups

Sport	Participation Rate of Ethnic Minority Groups	National Average Participation Rate
Gymnastics	Black African (3%)	1%
Track and field athletics	Black African (2%)	Less than 1%
Self-defence martial arts	Chinese (3%)	Less than 1%

A similarly complex picture is painted when you look at coaching, as illustrated in the examples below:

- There are very few female coaches at an elite level from all sections of society.
- From the Moscow Olympics in 1980 to the Sydney Olympics in 2000, the number of female coaches within the British team fell from 9% to 7.6%, despite the rise in the number of female athletes competing.
- In terms of female participants from ethnic minorities at the Olympics, it is easy to think of some high-profile black female athletes (eg Denise Lewis, Donna Fraser, Kelly Holmes). However, it is much more difficult to think of any high-profile black female coaches.
- Only five of the Women's Football League Premier clubs are managed by women.
- There are very few disabled coaches and there is an assumption that the ones there are can only coach disabled participants.

It is important to recognise that certain groups of people may be excluded from your sport, whether intentionally or not. Use national population statistics as a general guide to gauge how equitable your coaching sessions are. However, remember that they only reflect the national average and that you also need to bear in mind the huge regional/local variations that can occur. For example, in 1996, the ethnic minority population in London was 26%, in the West Midlands 10% and in the South West 1%[1].

Try to find out about the population statistics in your area – the following organisations should be able to provide relevant information:

- Local council
- General Register Office for Scotland
- Northern Ireland Statistics and Research Agency
- Office for National Statistics (England and Wales).

See pages 115 and 116 for contact details.

Access

As a coach, you have a responsibility to ensure that disabled people, people from ethnic minorities and women and girls have the same access to your coaching sessions as everyone else, within the context of their ability and activity at all levels. Your coaching sessions should be open, fair and accessible to all the sections of the community that they cater for. You need to recognise that some groups of people will require more encouragement and support to get involved in sport and that some may require specialist equipment and training. However, this should not deter you from taking positive action to include the key target groups in your coaching sessions.

Fairness

You must treat all participants equally, but at the same time be aware that some people may need more support than others. It is also important to recognise that different people have different needs and aspirations.

Taking Action

Sport plays a major role in promoting the inclusion of all groups of people in society. As a coach, you play an important part in this social inclusion because of your role in providing sporting opportunities at all levels of participation, from beginner to elite level. You have a responsibility to take positive action to ensure that your sport becomes equally accessible to everyone in society. This might seem a daunting prospect at the moment, but by the end of this pack, you should feel more confident and better equipped to do this.

1 *Source of statistics:* Sport England (2000) ***Making English sport inclusive: equity guidelines for governing bodies.*** London, Sport England. Ref no: SE/1043/1M/6/00

Code of Practice for Sports Coaches

sports coach UK has developed a *Code of Practice for Sports Coaches* in order to establish, publicise and maintain standards of ethical behaviour in coaching practice, and to inform and protect members of the public using the services of sports coaches. The Code forms the Values Statement underpinning the National Occupational Standards for Coaching, Teaching and Instructing reviewed in 1997 by the National Training Organisation for Sport, Recreation and Allied Occupations (SPRITO).

The Code states that:

Coaches must respect the rights, dignity and worth of every human being and their ultimate right to self-determination. Specifically, coaches must treat everyone equitably and sensitively, within the context of their activity and ability, regardless of gender, ethnic origin, cultural background, sexual orientation, religion or political affiliation.

sports coach UK Code of Practice for Sports Coaches (2005)

The status of the coach continues to increase in the perception of the public at large and it is therefore crucial for you to adopt and abide by the Code, which reflects the highest standards of good coaching practice. In doing so, you accept your responsibility to:

- sports participants and their parents/families
- coaching and other colleagues
- your governing body
- your coaching employer
- society.

sports coach UK
The National Coaching Foundation

1 To obtain a copy of the Code and further information about **sports coach UK** Membership Services, contact **Coachwise 1st4sport** (see page 111 for contact details).

Legal Requirements

Providing sporting opportunities for everyone in society regardless of their ability, race and gender is not just a moral responsibility, but could also be a legal requirement in some instances, particularly for organisations deemed to be service providers (eg local authority, national governing body, sporting organisation). Several Acts of Parliament attempt to protect the rights of individuals in the areas of education, service provision or employment:

- Children Act 1989
- Code of Practice on the protection of the dignity of women and men at work (Commission of European Communities 90/C 157/02, 27.6.90s. 3.2)
- Disability Discrimination Act 1995
- Equal Pay Act 1970
- Health and Safety at Work 1974
- Human Rights Act 1998
- Northern Ireland Act 1998
- Occupiers Liability Act (revised 1985)
- Public Order Act 1940
- Race Relations Act 1976
- Race Relations (Amendment) Act 2000
- Race Relations (Northern Ireland) Order 1997
- Rehabilitation of Offenders Act 1974
- Scotland Act 1998
- Sex Discrimination Act 1975.

While all of the above apply as much to the sporting world as to other areas of life, the acts you particularly need to be aware of are:

- Disability Discrimination Act 1995
- Race Relations Act 1976 and Race Relations (Amendment) Act 2000
- Race Relations (Northern Ireland) Order 1997
- Sex Discrimination Act 1975
- Northern Ireland Act 1998
- Scotland Act 1998.

Section 6.1 provides a brief overview of each of the above Acts and will help you understand how they affect you and your coaching.

The Government has recognised the value of sport in promoting the inclusion of all groups of people in society and being used as part of programmes to reduce crime and anti-social behaviour. The Government agenda in relation to equity in society in general also applies to sport. As a result, many initiatives and organisations have been introduced to improve the sporting opportunities available to the key target groups.

Appendix B provides a summary of the key organisations and initiatives you should be aware of. It is divided into the following three sections:

- *Government Agenda* takes a look at key government initiatives designed to provide better sporting opportunities for the key target groups.
- *Sport Agenda* examines the progress made by key UK sports organisations.
- *Coaching Agenda* looks at coaching-specific initiatives.

Appendix B will help you look beyond the *bigger picture* of government policy and understand why sports equity in coaching is so important.

sports coach UK

1.4 Summary

This section should have helped you to understand the concept of sports equity and why it is so important. The key points you need to remember are listed in the panel below.

- The key elements of sports equity are:

Recognising inequalities	Acknowledging that certain groups of people are under-represented in all areas of sport.
Access	Providing sports opportunities for everyone within the context of their ability and activity.
Fairness	Treating all participants equally, but being aware that some people may need more support than others. Recognising that different people have different needs and aspirations.
Taking action	Taking positive action to ensure that your sport becomes equally accessible to everyone in society.

These **RAFT** elements relate very closely to your responsibilities as a coach.

- Many different groups of people are disadvantaged in sport. However, some groups experience discrimination on a more regular basis, not only in sport, but in their daily lives in general. This pack will therefore focus on the following key target groups:
  - Disabled people
  - People from ethnic minorities
  - Women and girls.
- Providing sporting opportunities for everyone, regardless of ability, race and gender, is not just a moral duty, it is also a legal requirement. The Acts of Parliament you particularly need to be aware of are:
  - Disability Discrimination Act 1995
  - Race Relations Act 1976 and Race Relations (Amendment) Act 2000
  - Race Relations (Northern Ireland) Order 1997
  - Sex Discrimination Act 1975
  - Northern Ireland Act 1998
  - Scotland Act 1998.

Ensuring your coaching sessions are as accessible as possible means encouraging the key target groups to attend. To do this, it is important to understand why they might be put off from doing so. Section Two looks at the barriers that may prevent the key target groups from participating in sport.

Section Two

Barriers to Participation

2.0 What's In It For You?

There are a variety of reasons why people could be put off attending your coaching sessions. This could be down to something either within or beyond your control. To ensure your coaching sessions are as accessible as possible, it is important to understand the barriers that might prevent the key target groups from participating.

Some barriers to participation apply to everyone, not just people from the key target groups. These include things like:

- lack of awareness of sports activities on offer due to poor marketing and promotion
- inconvenient times
- no spare time
- domestic/work commitments take priority
- inconvenient venues
- poor facilities
- lack of transport
- fear for personal safety getting to and from the venue
- too expensive
- previous negative experiences (eg bad memories of PE lessons at school)
- lack of motivation
- parental attitudes and influences.

However, some barriers are particularly relevant to people from the key target groups. This section is divided into three subsections, one for each of the key target groups. By the end of the section, you should be able to:

- explain the barriers to participation for each key target group
- identify the barriers to participation in specific coaching scenarios.

2.1 Disabled People

The following panel identifies the key issues that may act as barriers to disabled people participating in sport.

BARRIERS TO PARTICIPATION IN SPORT

Assumptions

- Assumption that disabled people only take part in sport for therapeutic reasons. However, many take part for the same reasons as non-disabled people.
- Assumptions about which sports disabled people are interested in.
- Assumptions about which sports disabled people can and cannot participate in.
- Assumptions about what disabled people can and cannot do.
- Assumption that disabled people can't be integrated into coaching sessions for non-disabled people and that separate sessions need to be provided.

Lack of Informed Coaches

- Lack of coaches who are appropriately trained and informed about coaching disabled people.
- Lack of understanding about the different needs of different impairment groups.
- Lack of competitive opportunities.

Poor Communication

- Poor communication – this includes failure to:
  - consult directly with disabled people to find out about their needs and aspirations
  - advertise sports opportunities for disabled people adequately and appropriately, and in places they regularly go to (eg day centres, special schools, youth clubs)
  - provide adequate encouragement – some disabled people have low self-esteem and need more than just an advertisement to encourage them to take part in sport
- Use of inappropriate language.

Poor Facilities

- Lack of access to and within venues.
- Inadequate changing facilities.
- Lack of specialist equipment.

Poor Timing

- Coaching sessions run at inconvenient times (eg off-peak).

The following scenarios describe two different coaching situations. As you read through them, try to identify whether the organisation/coach could have done more to make their coaching sessions more accessible to disabled people.

Scenario 4

A local voluntary organisation wants to hold a *Come and Try It!* sports day for disabled people. They choose a venue because it is relatively cheap to hire for the day, although it is a bit out of the way on the outskirts of town and isn't on any major bus routes. They ask local sports clubs to hold hourly coaching sessions in their sport for any disabled people that turn up to the session.

The organisation sends letters to local schools and colleges, inviting disabled pupils to come to the *Come and Try It!* day and have a go at some of the activities on offer.

Do you think the organisation would attract many disabled people to the *Come and Try It* day?

Scenario 5

A local leisure centre runs a judo club for young people every Tuesday evening. The club is both popular and successful, with many members doing well at local competitions.

Most of the club members attend a local school, where there are a number of disabled pupils. Several of the disabled pupils are keen to join the club, but because it is so popular, there are no places left for new members, with or without disabilities.

The club coach therefore starts up a second club night at the leisure centre and divides the new and existing members between the two nights according to level of ability, not disability. Realising that she will need help to run both club nights, she contacts members of the senior judo club to find out if anyone is interested in getting involved in coaching. She plans to encourage any coaches who come forward to work towards the British Judo Association Preliminary Club Coach Award (if they've not already got it) and to attend the **sports coach UK** workshop *Coaching Disabled Performers.*

Do you think the judo coach would succeed in making her club accessible to disabled people?

As you read through the feedback below, try to relate it to your own situation and think about how you could make your coaching sessions more accessible to disabled people.

Scenario 4

The organisation would have been unlikely to attract many disabled people to the *Come and Try It!* day for the following reasons:

- Many people who were invited to the event might have been fed up with this kind of *Come and Try It!* day and would have preferred the opportunity to become a member of a sports club.
- Cost took priority over accessibility when the venue for the *Come and Try It!* day was selected. Because of this, it wasn't very easy for people to get to, which explains why attendance was far lower than expected.
- Not only was the venue difficult to get to in the first place, the building itself may not have catered particularly well for people with disabilities, for example:
  - no car park nearby
  - poor access and facilities for people in wheelchairs
  - no hearing induction loops.
- Given the choice, the disabled pupils might have preferred to try different sports to those on offer.
- The organisers and coaches might not have been sufficiently trained or informed about coaching disabled people and therefore didn't take into account the different needs of different impairment groups.
- The appropriate equipment may not have been available.

Had the voluntary organisation consulted all the parties involved in the *Come and Try It!* day prior to making definite arrangements, many of the problems listed above could have been avoided.

sports coach UK

Scenario 5

The judo coach would have been likely to succeed in making her club accessible to disabled people for the following reasons:

- She arranges an additional club night, rather than just saying the club is full and can't accommodate any new members.
- She divides new and existing members between the two club nights by ability, not disability, rather than running separate club nights for non-disabled and disabled members.
- She contacts the senior judo club to identify potential new coaches to help her run the two club nights. Increasing the number of coaches at the club night will mean that the coach-participant ratio is lower and that members will receive more individual attention.
- She helps senior judo club members work towards a recognised coaching award in judo. This will ensure that all the club's coaches operate in line with the recommended good practice advocated by the British Judo Association.
- She arranges for all club coaches to receive training on coaching disabled people. This will ensure they understand the needs of the club members who are disabled and that they are able to adapt their coaching methods to support them.

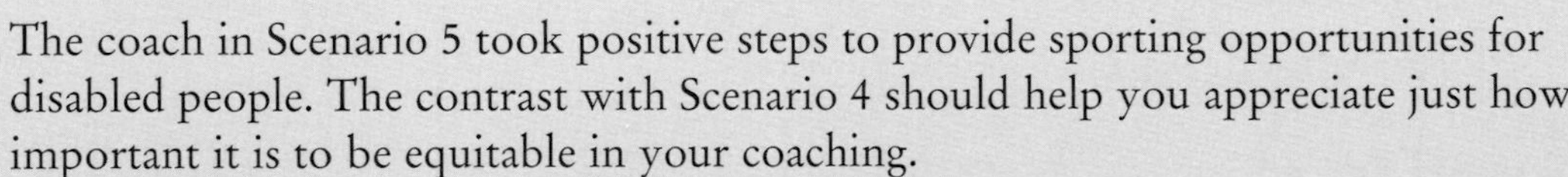

The coach in Scenario 5 took positive steps to provide sporting opportunities for disabled people. The contrast with Scenario 4 should help you appreciate just how important it is to be equitable in your coaching.

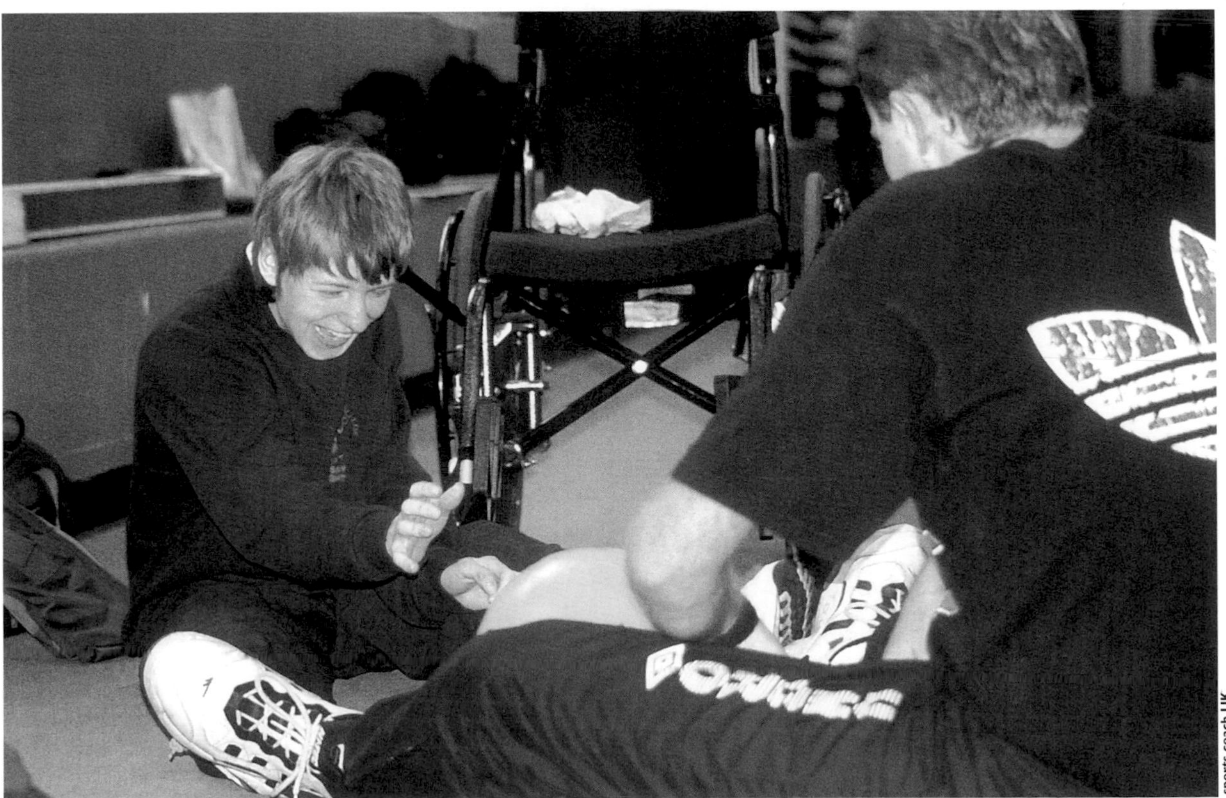

sports coach UK

2.2 People from Ethnic Minorities

The following panel identifies the key issues that may act as barriers to people from ethnic minorities participating in sport.

BARRIERS TO PARTICIPATION IN SPORT

Cultural/religious Influences

- Religious beliefs – for example, it may not be possible to:
  - wear specified sports kit
  - attend coaching sessions during religious festivals or at times reserved for prayer.

See Appendix C for further information about religious festivals.

- Lack of single gender coaching sessions with coach of appropriate gender.
- Lack of privacy in changing areas.
- Lack of parental support – Asian girls in particular may experience stricter parental control, which prevents them from participating in out-of-home leisure activities.
- Sport is often viewed as a *luxury* pastime with little relevance to everyday life.

Fear of Discrimination

- Fear of being stereotyped and discriminated against – people from ethnic minorities are often stereotyped into certain sports.
- Fear of racial abuse or attacks.

Low Self-esteem

- Lack of confidence and feeling self-conscious.
- Negative past experiences (eg at school).
- Having no-one to go with.
- Lack of positive images and role models.

Poor Communication

- Use of inappropriate language.
- Inadequate advertising of sports activities available in appropriate places (eg community centres).

Practicalities

- Cost.
- Lack of time.
- Lack of transport.

Unwelcoming Environment at Sports Centre

- Sports facilities often seen as *mainstream* (ie for white communities).
- A feeling of not belonging.
- Unsympathetic staff.
- Language barriers.

The following scenarios describe two different coaching situations. As you read through them, try to identify whether the coaches could have done more to make their coaching sessions more accessible to people from ethnic minorities.

Scenario 6

A rugby coach decides to hold an open evening to encourage more young people from ethnic minorities to join his club. He sets a date and produces the following flyer to advertise the event:

He distributes the flyer to local shops and the PE department at the local comprehensive school, and leaves some at the club's reception.

Do you think the rugby coach would attract many young people from ethnic minorities to the open evening?

Come
and have a go at rugby – join our scrum!

When?
Monday 5 March 2001

Where?
Anytown Rugby Club

Time?
7:00–9:00pm

Scenario 7

A coach runs junior sessions at a hockey club. Most of the girls that attend the sessions come from outside the local area and, although the coach doesn't have a problem with this, she also wants to encourage more local girls, most of whom are from ethnic minorities, to take part. She contacts local community leaders for advice on how to do this. They provide her with the information she needs and give their seal of approval to her plans.

The coach produces a promotional flyer to advertise the hockey sessions and circulates it round the local community via local schools, community centres, Racial Equality Councils and community groups. The flyer contains:

- background information about the club
- details of the days and times at which junior sessions are held
- details of the cost of the coaching session and concessionary rates made available by the local authority leisure department
- a message of support from the local community leaders.

The coach invites girls and their parents/carers to come and watch one of the sessions and meet the other female coaches who help to run them. She emphasises that it isn't necessary to wear any particular kind of clothing or shoes to take part in the coaching sessions, as long as they are comfortable, suitable and safe.

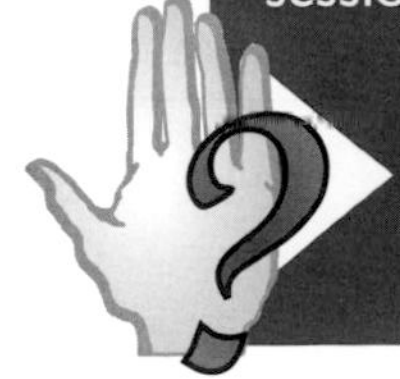

Do you think the coach would attract many girls from ethnic minorities to her hockey sessions?

As you read through the feedback below, try to relate it to your own situation and think about how you could make your coaching sessions more accessible to people from ethnic minorities.

Scenario 6

The rugby coach would have been unlikely to attract many young people from ethnic minorities to his open evening for the following reasons:

- He didn't liaise or consult with anyone from the local ethnic minority community about:
  - where the open evening was held
  - whether the date was suitable
  - whether the time was suitable
  - any other requirements people may have
  - the best way to promote the open evening.

  If he had, he would have found out that:
  - young people would have been more likely to go to the open evening if it had been held at the local community centre rather than the usual club venue
  - the date clashed with Eid-ul Fitr, an important Muslim festival that would prevent some potential participants from attending the open evening
  - the communal changing facilities at the club would put people off
  - local community leaders could have advertised the open evening on his behalf – the fact that they were supporting the event would have shown potential participants and their parents/carers that the club was serious about encouraging them to attend.
- He didn't explain that potential participants wouldn't need to wear special sports kit or that all necessary equipment would be provided.
- He didn't provide any information about the coaches that would be running the open evening (ie whether there would be both male and female coaches).
- He didn't include the cost (if any) of the open evening in his advert.
- The advert included a photo of a white rugby player – using a photo of players from ethnic minorities instead might have encouraged more people to attend the open evening.
- The open evening wasn't very well advertised.

Scenario 7

The coach would have been likely to succeed in making her hockey club accessible to all girls in the local area, regardless of ethnic origin, for the following reasons:

- She recognises that, although the majority of the girls in the local area are from ethnic minorities, very few attend her hockey sessions.
- Rather than assume that this is because they simply aren't interested in hockey, she realises that many of them may either be unaware that the hockey club exists or would find it too daunting to join.
- She contacts local community leaders for advice on how to encourage girls from ethnic minorities to attend her club and gets their seal of approval for her plan.
- She advertises the hockey sessions in places that local girls regularly go to.
- She recognises the barriers that might prevent girls from ethnic minorities attending the sessions and makes sure that the promotional flyer provides adequate reassurance:
  - She realises they might have never heard of the club, so she provides a bit of background information, together with the days and times of the junior sessions.
  - She keeps the cost of the coaching sessions to a minimum and agrees concessionary rates for people on low income with the local authority.
  - She realises that parents/carers might be worried about allowing their daughters to attend the sessions, so she invites them to come along with their daughters to watch a session and meet the coaches.
  - She realises that, due to religious or cultural reasons, it may not be appropriate for girls from ethnic minorities to attend coaching sessions run by male coaches, so she ensures that the sessions are run by female coaches.
  - Similarly, she realises that, due to religious or cultural reasons, girls from ethnic minorities may not be able to wear certain kinds of clothing, so she emphasises that they can wear whatever they like, providing it is comfortable, suitable and safe.

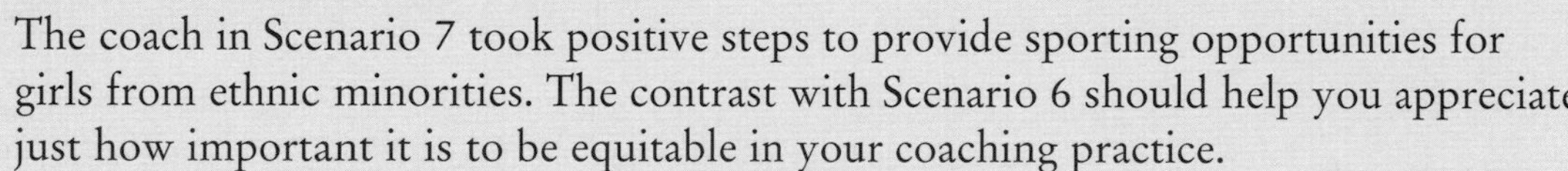

The coach in Scenario 7 took positive steps to provide sporting opportunities for girls from ethnic minorities. The contrast with Scenario 6 should help you appreciate just how important it is to be equitable in your coaching practice.

2.3 Women and Girls

The following panel identifies the key issues that may act as barriers to women and girls participating in sport.

BARRIERS TO PARTICIPATION IN SPORT

Attitudes of Others

- Indifference or negative attitude of some sporting organisations.
- Peer group pressure.
- Lack of female coaches.

Inconvenient Venue

- Lack of transport.
- Fear for personal safety getting to and from venue.
- Lack of quality childcare facilities.

Other Commitments

- Domestic/work commitments have to take priority.
- Too many conflicting interests.

Low Self-esteem

- Lack of confidence.
- Low expectations.

Poor Communication

- Use of inappropriate language.
- Poor media coverage of women's sport.

sports coach UK

The following scenarios describe two different coaching situations. As you read through them, try to identify whether the coaches could have done more to make their coaching sessions more accessible to women and girls.

Scenario 8

Shiretown Leisure Centre is situated in the middle of a large industrial town. The centre was built about twenty years ago and has had the same manager all this time. He will be retiring in the next year or so and makes no secret of the fact that he can't wait to leave.

The centre is showing signs of wear and tear as the local authority have not had much money available to spend on it in recent years. A new leisure centre has been built at the edge of the town. It is modern and clean, with all the latest equipment and facilities, and a new, enthusiastic manager. The more forward-looking staff from the old centre have already got jobs at the new leisure centre, leaving the old centre short-staffed.

Tom is a self-employed football coach and is keen to encourage more women to play football. He decides to book the sports hall at the old leisure centre on Sunday evenings to run women's football sessions. He chooses the old leisure centre over the new one because it is cheaper and nearer to where he lives. He decides to run the sessions from 8:00–9:00pm as he is free at that time each week.

Tom designs a poster to advertise the football sessions

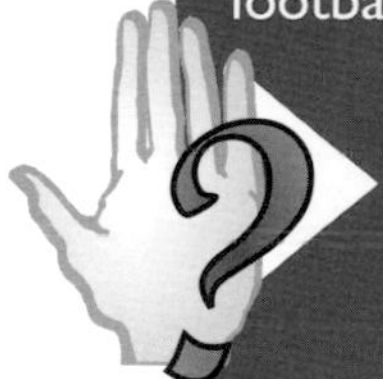

Do you think Tom would attract many women to his football sessions?

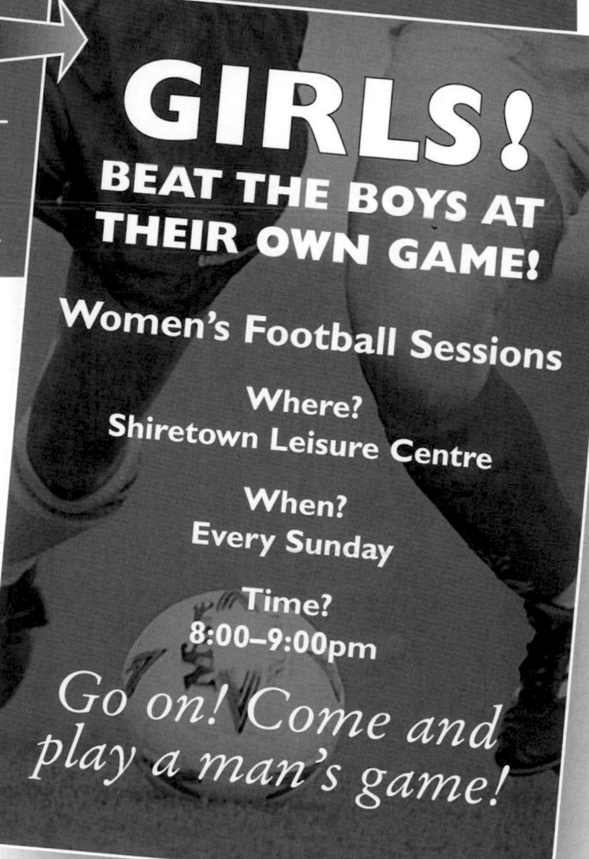

Scenario 9

A cricket coach is specifically responsible for drawing up training programmes for all new members at her club. She always meets new members individually and tries to make sure that the training programmes she subsequently comes up with complement their lifestyle and other commitments. She also provides them with a list of essential equipment they will need and explains that, if they like, a more experienced cricketer will be assigned to them to provide guidance and support.

While her general approach is the same for both male and female athletes, she recognises that there are specific things to bear in mind when preparing training programmes for female participants. The kinds of questions she asks new female members include:

- How many hours a week can they realistically devote to their training?
- When are the best times for them to train?
- How will they get to the club (eg own car, get a lift, public transport)?
- Training sessions may take place at other venues – would this be a problem?
- Would they prefer to attend mixed or women-only training sessions?
- Would they prefer to attend training sessions run by a male or female coach?
- Would they be interested in using the club crèche?
- Do they have any other requirements?

Do you think the cricket coach would succeed in making her club accessible to women?

As you read through the feedback below, try to relate it to your own situation and think about how you could make your coaching sessions more accessible to women and girls.

Scenario 8

Tom would have been unlikely to attract many women to his football sessions for the following reasons:

- Not many women were aware of the football sessions because they were only advertised at the leisure centre, which many had never been to before.
- The poster implied that football is a male reserve.
- Tom assumed that all women would jump at the chance of being able to play football when, in actual fact, they were more interested in other sports.
- The poster was offensive – this reflected on Tom both as a man and a coach, and several women decided that, although they quite fancied having a go at football, they didn't want to be coached by him.
- The poster didn't mention how much the sessions cost or whether equipment would be provided.
- The time of the session wasn't particularly convenient for most women.

- Many women didn't like being in the centre of town at that time of night.
- Public transport was practically non-existent on Sunday evenings.
- The leisure centre doesn't have a very welcoming environment:
  - The changing rooms aren't very clean.
  - The car park is badly lit at night.
  - The leisure centre manager isn't particularly welcoming or enthusiastic.
  - The leisure staff are overworked and take this out on the customers.
  - There are no childcare facilities.

Scenario 9

The cricket coach would have been likely to succeed in making her club accessible to women for the following reasons:

- She treats all new male and female club members equally. Women might be particularly reassured by the fact that they don't need to fork out on lots of new equipment straight away and that they have the opportunity to receive guidance from a more experienced cricketer.
- In addition, she realises there are special issues to consider when devising training programmes for women and therefore finds out as much as she can about their requirements beforehand. This includes finding out:
  - how much time women can devote to training and what the best times to train are – they often have other work and domestic commitments that have to take priority, so it is important that training times are convenient
  - how they will get to the club and making them aware that training sessions may be held at different venues, as it is important that all venues are convenient and safe to get to
  - whether they would prefer to attend mixed or women-only training sessions led by male or female coaches, as some women may feel more comfortable at women-only sessions run by a female coach
  - whether it would help if a crèche were available at the time of the training sessions, as this might be an important factor that influences women to continue their membership of the club
  - whether they have any other requirements, as it is important that the training programme caters for these.

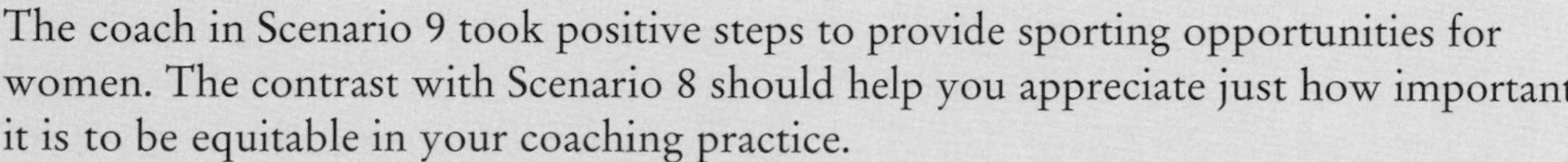

The coach in Scenario 9 took positive steps to provide sporting opportunities for women. The contrast with Scenario 8 should help you appreciate just how important it is to be equitable in your coaching practice.

2.4 Summary

Although certain barriers to participation apply only to a specific target group, you will have noticed that many are common to all the key target groups. The diagram on the next page should help you remember what these are.

The coaches in Scenarios 5 (page 15), 7 (page 19) and 9 (page 24) made every effort to be fair to everyone who wanted to be involved in their sport. This meant extra effort in some areas (eg arranging an additional judo club night) and relaxing rules in others (eg allowing girls at the netball club to wear whatever clothing they feel most comfortable in). In all three scenarios, this may have resulted in more people being involved in sport.

You should aim to put the same effort into your coaching practice. Don't worry if this seems a daunting prospect, the rest of this pack will help you make your coaching sessions more accessible to the key target groups. Section Three starts by looking at the appropriate language and terminology to use when talking or referring to the key target groups.

sports coach UK

SPORT

COACH

ASSUMPTIONS	LACK OF KNOWLEDGE	POOR COMMUNICATION
• Which sports people are interested in • Which sports people are able to do • People's reasons for taking part in sport	• Indifference/negative attitudes • Lack of encouragement • Lack of understanding of needs and aspirations • Lack of skills	• Lack of communication with key target groups and organisations that can help • Inappropriate language • Inappropriate and inadequate marketing • Lack of positive role models

FACILITIES

INCONVENIENCE	LACK OF TRANSPORT	SAFETY FEARS	INADEQUATE FACILITIES AND EQUIPMENT

COST

SESSION FEE	KIT AND EQUIPMENT

TIME

INCONVENIENCE	OTHER COMMITMENTS • Work • Domestic • Other interests

PERSONAL ISSUES

LOW SELF-ESTEEM	FEAR OF DISCRIMINATION AND UNWELCOMING ENVIRONMENT	CULTURAL/ RELIGIOUS INFLUENCES

PARTICIPATION

Action Plus

Section Three

Language and Terminology

3.0 What's In It For You?

In any coaching situation, it is important to treat your participants fairly and with respect – language has a vital role to play in this. In order to create a positive, welcoming coaching environment, it is vital that the language you use is:

- sensitive
- appropriate
- relevant.

Language is continually evolving as awareness and attitudes change. For example, several words used in the context of disability, which were acceptable in the past, are now no longer used. *Spastic* used to be a common term, but has now been replaced by *person with cerebral palsy*. This was mainly due to the misuse of the term, which subsequently became one of ridicule.

By the end of this section, you should be:

- aware of the appropriate terminology to use when referring to people from each of the key target groups, both during and outside your coaching sessions
- able to identify examples of acceptable and unacceptable terminology.

The information in this section is by no means exhaustive, nor a definitive guide – the terms included here may be revised or disappear in the future and other terms may appear.

3.1 Disabled People

The following table contains some of the common terms associated with disability. The left-hand column lists terms used in the past, which should now be avoided; the right-hand column lists more acceptable alternatives. Some of the terms are also mentioned in Appendix D.

Unacceptable	Acceptable
the blind	blind and partially sighted people/ visually impaired people
the deaf/hard of hearing/ profoundly deaf	deaf or hard of hearing people/ people with a hearing impairment
deaf and dumb	deaf without speech
the disabled/the handicapped/ cripples/invalids	disabled people/people with disabilities
disabled toilets	accessible toilets
dumb/mute	person with a speech impairment/ speech impaired person
an epileptic	person with epilepsy
handicap	disability/impairment
mentally disabled/subnormal/ abnormal/retarded/backward	person with learning disabilities
Mongolism	Down's Syndrome
normal people/able-bodied people	non-disabled people
patient	person
spastic	person with cerebral palsy
special needs	(additional) needs
wheelchair bound/ confined to a wheelchair	wheelchair user
wheelchair coach	coach
victim of/stricken by/crippled by/ afflicted by/sufferer of	has/with (the particular condition)

3.2 People from Ethnic Minorities

As with terms relating to disability, many of those associated with people from ethnic minorities should be avoided, even if they were regarded as acceptable in the past. Examples include:

Term	Reasons to Avoid
Coloured	Regarded as outdated and generally offensive to many black people. When applied to South Africa, the term reflects issues of ethnic divide and apartheid.
Half-caste	Regarded as outdated and racist.
Non-white	Implies that *white* is the generic term for all people.
Paki	An offensive and derogatory term often used to refer to people from Pakistan or Asian people in general.

Based on information provided on the British Sociological Association website (www.britsoc.org.uk)

sports coach UK

You should always use more acceptable terminology when referring to people from ethnic minorities. The most common terms you need to be aware of include:

Term	Guidance
People from ethnic minorities	Use this term when referring collectively to people of different ethnic origin and background.
Black people	Use this term when referring to people of African, Caribbean and South Asian origin. However, remember that some Asian groups in Britain object to being referred to as *black*; some people believe the term confuses a number of ethnic groups, which should be treated separately. One solution to this is to refer to *black* ***peoples*** *or black* ***communities*** in the plural to imply that there is a variety of such groups. You should also be aware that *black* can also be used in a racist sense in certain contexts[1].
Asian people	Use this term when referring to people from the Asian sub-continent – India, Pakistan, Bangladesh and Kashmir. Bear in mind that some people may prefer to refer to their country of origin (eg Bangladeshi, Indian, Pakistani) rather than to the general term Asian, which includes a wide variety of different cultural and ethnic groups. Other people may prefer to be referred to neither as Asian nor by their country of origin if several generations of their family have been living in Britain[2].

A more detailed list of terminology associated with people from ethnic minorities is provided in Appendix E.

1 and 2 Based on information provided on the British Sociological Association website (www.britsoc.org.uk)

3.3 Women and Girls

Although often unintentional, many people refer or talk to women and girls using terms which are sometimes perceived as patronising and offensive. The table below shows which terms to avoid, together with more acceptable alternatives.

Context	Avoid	Use
Referring/talking to a group of female participants	Birds/chicks/girls/ladies	Everyone/everybody/ women/females
Referring/talking to an individual female participant	Bird/chick/dear/ duck/love/pet	Name the participant wants to be known by/woman/female

Note: Not everyone will find the terms in the *Avoid* column patronising and offensive – some people may be quite happy for you to use them. Use your discretion when talking or referring to women and girls in your coaching sessions – if in doubt, ask participants how they would prefer to be addressed.

3.4 Summary

You should now be familiar with which terms to use and which to avoid when talking or referring to people from the key target groups. The next activity asks you to identify examples of acceptable and unacceptable terminology.

Supersport Photographs

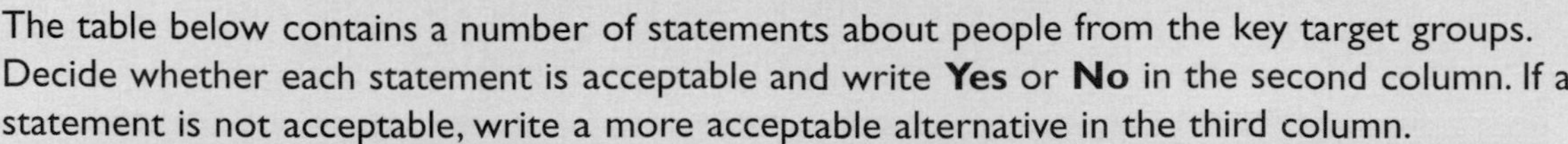

ACTIVITY 2

The table below contains a number of statements about people from the key target groups. Decide whether each statement is acceptable and write **Yes** or **No** in the second column. If a statement is not acceptable, write a more acceptable alternative in the third column.

Statement	Acceptable?	More Acceptable Alternative (if appropriate)
1 Harpal runs coaching sessions for both able-bodied and disabled gymnasts.		
2 Tony is a swimming coach, aiming to encourage more non-white people in the local area to take up swimming.		
3 Sophie contacts her governing body to find out more about coaching participants suffering from Down's Syndrome.		
4 Matthew makes sure his coaching venue has accessible toilets for wheelchair users.		
5 Daniel is asked to coach a women's rugby team. He declines saying he 'doesn't think rugby is a birds' game'.		
6 Nawal is asked to start coaching a group of mentally disabled teenagers who are interested in taking up badminton.		

Statement	Acceptable?	More Acceptable Alternative (if appropriate)
7 Hassiba runs basketball coaching sessions at her local community centre specifically aimed at women and girls from black and Asian communities.		
8 Desmond contacts British Blind Sport for information on modifying sports for visually impaired people.		
9 Carla is a wheelchair tennis coach.		
10 'Okay Sandra – can you return to your half of the court and prepare to serve again?' asked the squash coach.		

Now turn over.

Feedback

Statement	Acceptable?	More Acceptable Alternative (if appropriate)
1 *Harpal runs coaching sessions for both able-bodied and disabled gymnasts.*	*NO*	• *Harpal runs coaching sessions for both* ***non-disabled*** *and disabled gymnasts.* • *Harpal runs coaching sessions for* ***gymnasts of all abilities.***
2 *Tony is a swimming coach, aiming to encourage more non-white people in the local area to take up swimming.*	*NO*	*Tony is a swimming coach, aiming to encourage more* ***people from local ethnic minority communities*** *to take up swimming.*
3 *Sophie contacts her governing body to find out more about coaching participants suffering from Down's Syndrome.*	*NO*	*Sophie contacts her governing body to find out more about coaching participants* ***who have/with*** *Down's Syndrome.*
4 *Matthew makes sure his coaching venue has accessible toilets for wheelchair users.*	*YES*	*It is appropriate to refer to* ***accessible toilets*** *and* ***wheelchair users.***
5 *Daniel is asked to coach a women's rugby team. He declines saying he 'doesn't think rugby is a birds' game'.*	*NO*	*Not only is Daniel wrong to refer to women as 'birds', but he is also wrong to suggest that women cannot and should not play rugby!*
6 *Nawal is asked to start coaching a group of mentally disabled teenagers who are interested in taking up badminton.*	*NO*	*Nawal is asked to start coaching a group of teenagers* ***with learning disabilities.***
7 *Hassiba runs basketball coaching sessions at her local community centre specifically aimed at women and girls from black and Asian communities.*	*YES*	*It is appropriate to refer to* ***black and Asian communities.***

Statement	Acceptable?	More Acceptable Alternative (if appropriate)
8 Desmond contacts British Blind Sport for information on modifying sports for visually impaired people.	*YES*	*It is appropriate to refer to* ***visually impaired people.***
9 Carla is a wheelchair tennis coach.	*NO*	*Carla is a* ***tennis*** *coach.*
10 'Okay Sandra – can you return to your half of the court and prepare to serve again?' asked the squash coach.	*YES*	*It is appropriate to address any participant by the name by which they wish to be known.*

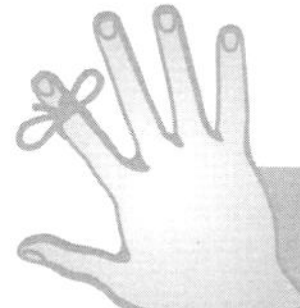

Remember!

- Use language that is sensitive, appropriate and relevant.
- Conversation between friends is different to conversation with people you don't know well.
- If you are unsure which terms are acceptable or unacceptable, ask the people you are coaching.
- Everybody has the right to choose how they wish to be referred to – not everyone may choose to be referred to in the same way.
- If someone refers to themselves in a way you find offensive, you don't have to use that word just because they do.

sports coach UK

Language and Terminology

Using appropriate language and terminology is just one way of ensuring your coaching sessions are as equitable as possible. Section Four looks at ways of applying and extending your existing coaching skills and experience to meet the needs of your participants.

sports coach UK

Section Four

Tips for More Equitable Coaching

4.0 What's In It For You?

You may find the prospect of coaching the key target groups in your sport a bit daunting, particularly if you don't have much previous experience. But it's not a case of having to learn a whole new set of a coaching skills, it's more about ***applying*** and ***extending*** your existing skills and experience to meet the needs of your participants. *Applying your existing skills* means treating the key target groups the same as you would any other participants – that is:

- communicating effectively
- planning coaching sessions and programmes to meet the needs of participants
- analysing and evaluating performance
- creating a safe environment
- being open-minded in developing your coaching skills and knowledge.

Extending your skills means understanding the additional issues you need to consider when coaching disabled people, people from ethnic minorities and women and girls.

By the end of this section, you should be:

- aware of the specific issues you need to consider when coaching the key target groups
- able to identify ways in which coaches make their sessions accessible and appropriate for the key target groups in specific coaching scenarios.

4.1 Disabled People

DON'T MAKE ASSUMPTIONS

- Don't assume that, just because not many disabled people currently attend your coaching sessions, they simply aren't interested in your sport. Think back to the barriers to participation identified in Section 2.1.
- Don't assume that disabled people just take part in sport because it's therapeutic. They participate in sport for the same reasons as non-disabled people (eg improve fitness, make friends, personal challenge, competition). The benefits of sport are also the same (eg improve confidence and self-esteem, handle pressure and stress).
- Don't make too many assumptions about whether people can take part in your sport – you'll be surprised how easily most sports can be adapted and how many disabled people can be successful with appropriate support from their coach.
- Coaching disabled people doesn't necessarily mean providing separate coaching sessions – it is often possible to integrate disabled people into existing sessions.

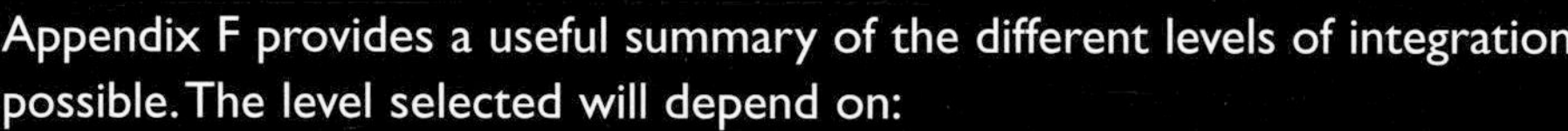

Appendix F provides a useful summary of the different levels of integration possible. The level selected will depend on:

- the type of sport
- the views of the disabled person
- your views
- the views of other participants
- the views of others (eg parents, helpers).

ACT APPROPRIATELY

- In order to create a positive, welcoming coaching environment, make sure you use language that is sensitive, appropriate and relevant, so as not to upset or offend disabled people. It can be difficult to know what is acceptable and unacceptable – refer back to Section Three for guidance.

COMMUNICATE

- Consulting your participants about their needs and aspirations is important, regardless of their ability. So as well as finding out about the broader issues associated with coaching disabled people, it's also important to consult disabled people individually about:
  - their specific needs
  - what kind of support they will need from you
  - what kind of specialist equipment they will need
  - existing skills and fitness levels
  - what they hope to achieve from the coaching sessions
  - other issues (eg transport, costs).
- Use language that is sensitive, appropriate and relevant both during and outside your coaching sessions (see Section 3.1 for more information).
- Effective communication is a key element of successful coaching. You may find there are additional challenges to the way you communicate when coaching disabled people. It is important that you establish the best way to communicate with individuals.

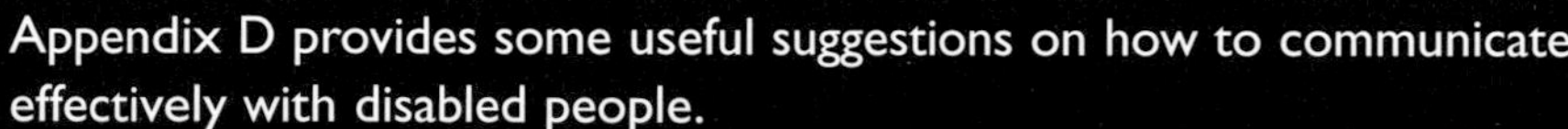

Appendix D provides some useful suggestions on how to communicate effectively with disabled people.

- Advertise your coaching sessions adequately, appropriately and in the right places (eg schools attended by disabled people). Include positive images of disabled people in any promotional material you produce. If required, provide promotional material in alternative formats (eg large print, audio).
- Encourage other coaches at your club to attend workshops/courses related to disability issues:

sports coach UK workshops:

- Equity in Your Coaching
- How to Coach Disabled People in Sport (Coaching Essentials Workshop)
- Coaching Disabled Performers (Develop Your Coaching Workshop)

Workshop dates and locations are available from the Business Support Centre.

See page 111 for contact details.

National governing body sport-specific courses

Many national governing bodies run courses designed to assist those working with disabled sportspeople. Find out what your national governing body has to offer.

Feedback

Shaheed makes his coaching sessions as equitable as possible by:

- *gaining information about coaching deaf and hearing impaired people (ie contacting the British Deaf Sports Council)*
- *attending appropriate coach education courses (ie* ***sports coach*** *UK and LTA workshops)*
- *communicating effectively and appropriately with his participants*
- *assessing the individual needs of his participants and adapting his existing coaching skills to meet them.*

Action Plus

4.2 People from Ethnic Minorities

DON'T MAKE ASSUMPTIONS

- Don't assume that, just because not many people from ethnic minorities currently attend your coaching sessions, they simply aren't interested in your sport. Think back to the barriers to participation identified in Section 2.2.
- Remember, the reasons people participate in sport are the same, regardless of ethnic origin (eg improve fitness, make friends, personal challenge, competition). The benefits of sport are also the same (eg improve confidence and self-esteem, handle pressure and stress). Try to raise awareness of these benefits – if possible, use positive role models from ethnic minorities.

COMMUNICATE

- Consult with relevant organisations and community leaders about issues such as:
  - appropriate venues, days and times for coaching sessions
  - specific requirements people from ethnic minorities may have
  - appropriate means of advertising your coaching sessions.

  Doing this will prove to people from ethnic minorities that you are serious about encouraging them to join your coaching sessions.
- Use language that is sensitive, appropriate and relevant both during and outside your coaching sessions (see Section 3.2 for more information).
- People from different ethnic backgrounds will have different needs and aspirations. It is therefore important to consult with individuals to find out about:
  - any specific requirements
  - what kind of support they will need from you
  - existing skills and fitness levels
  - what they hope to achieve from the coaching sessions
  - other issues (eg transport, costs).

  If you are coaching children and young people from ethnic minorities, don't forget to consult with their parents/carers too, to gain their support.
- Advertise your coaching sessions adequately and appropriately – make sure any promotional material you produce includes information that is relevant to people from ethnic minorities (eg clothing and equipment required, whether male and female coaches are available). Include positive images of people from ethnic minorities in any promotional material you produce.
- Encourage other coaches at your club to attend the **sports coach UK** workshop *Equity in Your Coaching*. Workshop dates and locations are available from the Business Support Centre.

See page 111 for contact details.

CATER FOR DIFFERENT NEEDS

- Be aware of different religious/cultural requirements, for example:
  - It may not be appropriate for women and girls from ethnic minorities to attend coaching sessions run by male coaches, so you would need to ensure that sessions run by female coaches are available.
  - It may be necessary to relax any club rules on clothing worn during coaching sessions. People from ethnic minorities are often required to wear certain items of clothing for religious/cultural reasons (eg turban). Similarly, they may be unable to wear certain kinds of clothing (eg sports skirt). Reassure participants that they can wear whatever they like, providing the clothing worn is comfortable, suitable and safe.
  - It may not be appropriate for people to take part in sport during important religious festivals. Appendix C provides a brief summary of the main festivals celebrated by people from different religions. You should always take these into account when scheduling coaching sessions, events or competitions. The list in Appendix C is not exhaustive, so remember to consult with individual participants too.
  - Be aware of other issues relating to religious festivals that may affect performance (eg fasting).
- Hold your coaching sessions at convenient venues. Don't just expect people to come to your club – try to run sessions within their community environment. Make sure the venues have adequate facilities that cater for the needs of people from ethnic minorities (eg cubicles rather than communal changing areas).
- Be prepared to adapt your coaching skills if necessary.

ACT APPROPRIATELY

- In order to create a positive, welcoming coaching environment, make sure you use language that is sensitive, appropriate and relevant, so as not to upset or offend people from ethnic minorities. It can be difficult to know what is acceptable and unacceptable – refer back to Section Three for guidance.

SEEK ADVICE

If in doubt, contact organisations that can offer help and advice.

See pages 112 to 117 for contact details.

Bear the information in the panels in mind as you complete the activity on page 48.

Action Plus

ACTIVITY 4

Read through the following scenario. As you do, try to identify ways in which Kath makes her coaching scheme accessible and appropriate for women and girls from ethnic minorities, and list them in the space provided on page 49.

Scenario 11

Kath is a coach at a local rowing club. She realises that very few women and girls from ethnic minorities are members of her club and wants to do something to encourage more to take up rowing.

She arranges to meet up with local community leaders to discuss her plan. In particular, she asks them about the barriers that might discourage women and girls from joining the club (eg cost, transport, time of coaching sessions, equipment required) and the best way to advertise the coaching scheme she intends to launch. The local community leaders think Kath's scheme is a great idea and say they will do everything they can to help her out. They put her in touch with a black female rower from the local area to feature as a positive role model in the promotional material Kath intends to produce.

Kath decides to run two sets of coaching sessions, one at the local community centre for those who would rather have a go at rowing on dry land before venturing onto the water and the other at a local lake for those who would rather go straight out onto the water. She enlists the help of other coaches from her rowing club, including two female coaches.

She produces a promotional flyer to advertise the coaching scheme, which includes the following information:

- Details of the two sets of coaching sessions on offer (ie one on dry land, the other on the water), with a note explaining that potential participants are free to swap to the other scheme after the introductory session if they wish.
- Details of the date, time and venue of the first sessions, with a note asking potential participants to let her know if these aren't convenient.
- Information about the cost of the coaching sessions – the first one will be free; subsequent ones heavily subsidised.
- Details of free transport available to and from the coaching venues.
- Names of the female coaches that will be helping Kath run the two schemes.
- Reassurance that all necessary equipment will be provided – all potential participants need to bring is themselves!
- Reassurance that no special kit needs to be worn – as long as it's suitable and safe for rowing in, potential participants can wear whatever they feel most comfortable in.
- A message of encouragement from the local community leaders and local black female rower.

Kath distributes the promotional flyers via routes identified by the local community leaders (eg local community centres, inserted in local community free newspaper).

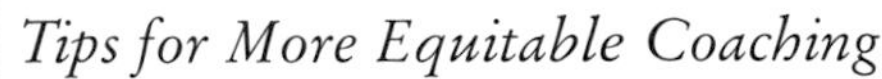

How does Kath make her coaching scheme accessible and appropriate for women and girls from ethnic minorities? List the reasons in the space provided below.

Now turn over.

Feedback

Kath makes her coaching sessions as equitable as possible by:

- *identifying that very few women and girls from ethnic minorities are members of her rowing club and deciding to do something to encourage more to take up rowing*
- *meeting and consulting with local community leaders to find out how best to tailor her rowing schemes to meet the needs of women and girls from ethnic minorities*
- *using a positive role model*
- *using local facilities and providing free transport*
- *trying to anticipate the most appropriate dates and times to run the coaching sessions, but asking potential participants to get back to her if these are inconvenient*
- *providing free/subsidised coaching sessions*
- *enlisting the help of other female coaches from ethnic minorities*
- *providing all necessary equipment*
- *having a relaxed dress code*
- *ensuring the promotional flyer includes the kind of information women and girls from ethnic minorities will want to know*
- *publicising the support of local community leaders and the positive role model*
- *distributing the promotional flyers via appropriate routes.*

Action Plus

4.3 Women and Girls

DON'T MAKE ASSUMPTIONS

- Don't assume that, just because not many women and girls currently attend your coaching sessions, they simply aren't interested in your sport. Think back to the barriers to participation identified in Section 2.3.
- Don't assume that all women and girls are interested in the same kinds of activities – offer as wide a choice as possible and tailor your coaching programmes to meet their different needs.
- Don't make assumptions about the capabilities of women and girls in your sport. All participants, regardless of gender, should be assessed individually to establish their current level of ability.

COMMUNICATE

- Consult women and girls to find out what sort of activities they are interested in (eg interviews, questionnaires).
- Use language that is sensitive, appropriate and relevant both during and outside your coaching sessions (see Section 3.3 for more information).
- Do not refer to a woman's marital status.
- Include positive images of women and girls in any promotional material you produce. These should reflect real women and girls in society, not just the model-like perfection frequently portrayed in women's magazines.
- Encourage other coaches at your club to attend the **sports coach UK** workshop *Equity in Your Coaching*. Workshop dates and locations are available from the Business Support Centre.

See page 111 for contact details.

CATER FOR DIFFERENT NEEDS

- Understand the barriers that may discourage women and girls from participating in sport, for example:
  - Many women and girls don't feel comfortable or confident at mixed sessions (eg fear of ridicule or abuse, don't want to look silly, worried about their appearance).
  - Many women and girls underestimate their levels of competency in sport and may think they aren't experienced or good enough to join your coaching sessions.
  - Personal safety is a particularly important issue for women and girls (eg transport, car park lighting, access to venue, timing).
- Understand the legal requirements under which you practice. Under the terms of sex discrimination legislation, it is only acceptable to run women-only coaching sessions if:
  - female participants are likely to suffer serious embarrassment at the presence of male participants
  - female participants are likely to be in a state of undress and might reasonably object to the presence of male participants
  - physical contact is likely between participants of the opposite sex and women and girls might reasonably object to this
  - coaching sessions are run by a single sex voluntary group.

  In all cases, you need to be able to justify running women-only sessions (eg expressed preferences from existing or potential participants, religious/cultural reasons, results of research/surveys). You may also need to restrict the running of coaching sessions to female coaches and consider allowing female spectators only or perhaps no spectators at all.

See page 83 for further information on the Sex Discrimination Act 1975.

- Be aware of the physiological differences between male and female participants of different ages that may affect performance (eg children's development, conditions that specifically affect female participants, such as osteoporosis or menstruation).
- Ensure your coaching sessions are held at easily accessible venues, which provide a welcoming environment for women and girls both in terms of staff and facilities.
- Although it may be difficult to find a time to suit everyone, establish the most convenient times for women to attend your coaching sessions. Women often have the same work commitments as men, so don't automatically assume you can run women's sessions during weekday off-peak periods only.
- Consider providing free or subsidised transport to and from your coaching sessions – this will benefit women and girls who would otherwise have difficulty getting to the venue as well as those who feel uncomfortable about travelling alone to coaching sessions.
- If your coaching venue doesn't already have one, consider providing a crèche for women bringing young children with them.
- Make sure your coaching sessions are reasonably priced, but remember that pricing policies must not discriminate between men and women. Female participants cannot be offered discounts that are not available to the same category of male participants.
- Consider alternatives to expensive equipment and kit (eg allowing a relaxed dress code).

ACT APPROPRIATELY

- In order to create a positive, welcoming coaching environment, make sure you use language that is sensitive, appropriate and relevant, so as not to upset or offend women and girls. It can be difficult to know what is acceptable and unacceptable – refer back to Section Three for guidance.
- During mixed coaching sessions:
  - use both male and female participants to demonstrate new skills
  - match participants by skill rather than gender when dividing them into pairs or small groups to learn new skills
  - check that participants feel comfortable about pair/group work with members of the opposite sex.
- As a general rule:
  - Refrain from over-familiarity and respect participants' individual space.
  - Never make comments or remarks of a sexual nature.
  - If some coaching techniques require physical contact or support, check your national governing body guidelines and ask the participant's permission first. Touching can be okay and appropriate, as long as it is neither intrusive nor disturbing.
  - Avoid going into changing facilities, especially while participants are getting changed. If it cannot be avoided, always ask participants' permission first.
  - Avoid spending time alone with individual participants.
  - Avoid giving participants a lift to and from coaching sessions in your car unless absolutely necessary, particularly if you are likely to be alone together.

SEEK ADVICE

If in doubt, contact organisations that can offer help and advice:

See pages 112 to 117 for contact details.

Bear the information in the panel in mind as you complete the next activity.

sports coach **UK**

ACTIVITY 5

Read through the following scenario. As you do, try to identify ways in which Jane makes her coaching sessions accessible and appropriate for both men and women, and list them in the space provided at the end of the scenario.

Scenario 12

Jane is a coach at a local cricket club. She decides to set up coaching sessions for beginners, which will be open to both men and women. She runs an introductory session to assess the existing skills of the participants. This includes drills and technique work in batting, bowling and fielding.

She starts off by observing the participants and later divides them up into pairs, matching similarly skilled players, having first made sure that the participants feel comfortable about working with members of the opposite sex.

When introducing new skills, Jane is as likely to ask a woman to demonstrate as she is to ask a man. She is sensitive in her use of language and uses both men and women as positive role models for particular coaching points.

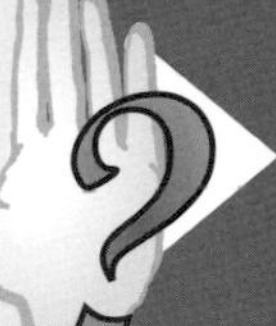

How does Jane make her coaching session accessible and appropriate for both male and female participants? List the reasons in the space provided below.

Now turn over.

Feedback

Jane makes her coaching session accessible and appropriate for both men and women by:

- *observing the participants to assess individual skill levels and technique*
- *checking that all participants feel comfortable about working with members of the opposite sex*
- *pairing similarly skilled players*
- *asking both men and women to demonstrate when introducing new skills*
- *being sensitive in her use of language*
- *using both men and women as positive role models.*

4.4 Summary

This section has identified ways to make your coaching sessions more accessible and appropriate for the key target groups. General points that apply to all the groups are shown in the diagram on page 57.

However, despite your best efforts to ensure that your coaching sessions are as equitable as possible, you cannot guarantee that everyone who attends them will behave in an equitable way. Section Five provides guidance on how to challenge the instances of inequitable behaviour that could arise during your coaching sessions.

Action Plus

Coach

DON'T MAKE ASSUMPTIONS ABOUT:

- which sports people are interested in
- which sports people are able to do
- people's reasons for taking part in sport – these are usually the same regardless of ability, ethnic origin or gender
- people's reasons for **not** taking part in sport – just because you may not currently coach many people from the key target groups doesn't mean they aren't interested in your sport

COMMUNICATE

- Consult people from the key target groups about their needs and aspirations
- Consult organisations that can help you meet the needs of the key target groups
- Use language that is sensitive, appropriate and relevant
- Advertise your coaching sessions adequately, appropriately and in the right places
- Encourage other coaches at your club to attend workshops relating to equity issues

CATER FOR DIFFERENT NEEDS

- Understand the barriers to participation that may put people off attending your coaching sessions
- Be aware of the needs and aspirations of people from the key target groups
- Identify safety and medical issues
- Hold your coaching sessions at convenient venues and times
- Keep the cost of your coaching sessions as low as possible

SEEK ADVICE

Contact organisations that can offer help and advice

See pages 112 to 117 for contact details.

Participation

sports coach UK

Section Five

Challenging Inequitable Behaviour

5.0 What's In It For You?

As a coach, you not only have a responsibility to behave equitably yourself, but you also play an important role in promoting equitable behaviour among your participants. It is important to recognise that, despite your best efforts to be a good role model, incidents of inequitable behaviour may arise during your coaching sessions.

By the end of this section, you should be able to:

- anticipate the kind of inequitable behaviour that could arise in your coaching sessions
- select appropriate ways of dealing with it.

Challenging inequitable behaviour doesn't mean adopting the role of *equity police* and judging participants' behaviour – remember, people may not be aware that the way they are behaving is unacceptable. Your role is to raise participants' awareness of sports equity issues and help them become more equitable.

5.1 Anticipating Inequitable Behaviour

Inequitable behaviour can be ***verbal, written*** or ***physical***. Examples of each type are shown in the table below.

Type of Inequitable Behaviour	Examples
Verbal	• Racist, sexist or homophobic language • Ridicule or bullying because of a personal characteristic (eg wearing glasses, being disabled)
Written	All of the above written down in some way (eg graffiti, in a letter, text messages on a mobile phone)
Physical	Action taken against somebody because of their race, gender, personal characteristic, sexuality. Examples include: • pushing • biting • tripping somebody up and pretending it is an accident • touching somebody inappropriately • stealing or destroying other people's property • excluding somebody from taking part in an activity.

sports coach UK

Inequitable behaviour can have a profound effect on the individual or groups of people it is directed against. This is highlighted in the example below.

In November 2000, the NSPCC published the results of major research[1] carried out to explore the childhood experience of young people in the UK, including their experience of abuse and neglect. The survey found that:

- 43% of the young people questioned identified bullying or being discriminated against by other children as the most common source of distress and misery
- bullying occurred mostly because of personal characteristics such as size, dress, race or manner of speech
- name-calling and verbal abuse were the most common forms of bullying
- 14–15% of the young people questioned were physically attacked
- many reported having had their property stolen or damaged.

The report concludes that for many children, the wider world of school, friends and community contains threats of bullying and discrimination and, for girls in particular, sexual harassment and violence.

Although it would be impossible to account for every eventuality, anticipating the kind of inequitable behaviour that could arise during your coaching sessions will mean you are better prepared to deal with any incidences that may occur. The next activity asks you to identify examples of inequitable behaviour from a list of coaching scenarios.

1 NSPCC (2000) ***Child maltreatment in the United Kingdom: a study of the prevalence of child abuse and neglect***. London, NSPCC.

ACTIVITY 6

1 Read through the following scenarios and decide which are examples of equitable and inequitable behaviour. Put a tick in the appropriate column to indicate your response.

2 If you decide a scenario is an example of inequitable behaviour, note what type it is – verbal, written or physical.

Scenario	Equitable	Inequitable
1 You are coaching a group of men and you hear one player telling the rest of the team that they are useless and playing like a bunch of girls.		
2 You find out that one of the children you coach has received a note signed by other team members telling her she's no longer wanted on the team because she's too fat.		
3 One of the players you coach scores a good goal and is congratulated by the rest of the team.		
4 You coach both men and women at your club. You notice that every time you coach two of the younger women, several of the men watch and make comments about the way they are dressed and other suggestive comments, which the women obviously find upsetting.		
5 You are told that some lesbian participants who attend your coaching sessions are frequently heard telling some of the young girls at the club that men are 'no good' and that they 'can't be trusted'.		
6 A member of the team you coach has not been involved in the sport for long. Other team members are supportive and always react positively to the efforts of the new member, even if it sometimes means they lose possession of the ball.		

Scenario	Equitable	Inequitable
7 Several of your club's members are from ethnic minorities. One day, one of these members draws your attention to a poster on the coaching notice board, which has been defaced with racist graffiti. You are given the name of the perpetrators, one of whom is a star player at the club.		
8 After a training session, you enter a changing room to see several young participants taunting another participant who wears glasses. One person even takes his glasses from him and stands on them.		
9 When asked to vote for the Player of the Year Award, the team you coach vote for a club member who is not the best player in the team, but is reliable, supportive and always turns up for training.		
10 You hear one of your participants telling another participant that he is playing 'like a spastic'.		

Now turn over.

Feedback

Compare your answers with those provided below:

Scenario	Equitable	Inequitable
1 *You are coaching a group of men and you hear one player telling the rest of the team that they are useless and playing like a bunch of girls.*		✓ *Verbal*
2 *You find out that one of the children you coach has received a note signed by other team members telling her she's no longer wanted on the team because she's too fat.*		✓ *Written*
3 *One of the players you coach scores a good goal and is congratulated by the rest of the team.*	✓	
4 *You coach both men and women at your club. You notice that every time you coach two of the younger women, several of the men watch and make comments about the way they are dressed and other suggestive comments, which the women obviously find upsetting.*		✓ *Verbal*
5 *You are told that some lesbian participants who attend your coaching sessions are frequently heard telling some of the young girls at the club that men are 'no good' and that they 'can't be trusted'.*		✓ *Verbal*
6 *A member of the team you coach has not been involved in the sport for long. Other team members are supportive and always react positively to the efforts of the new member, even if it sometimes means they lose possession of the ball.*	✓	

Scenario	Equitable	Inequitable
7 Several of your club's members are from ethnic minorities. One day, one of these members draws your attention to a poster on the coaching notice board, which has been defaced with racist graffiti. You are given the name of the perpetrators, one of whom is a star player at the club.		✓ *Written*
8 After a training session, you enter a changing room to see several young participants taunting another participant who wears glasses. One person even takes his glasses from him and stands on them.		✓ *Physical*
9 When asked to vote for the Player of the Year Award, the team you coach vote for a club member who is not the best player in the team, but is reliable, supportive and always turns up for training.	✓	
10 You hear one of your participants telling another participant that he is playing 'like a spastic'.		✓ *Verbal*

Action Plus

5.2 Dealing with Inequitable Behaviour

You should always challenge inequitable behaviour in a positive way. The panel below provides some useful points to bear in mind.

- Having a code of conduct will make it easier to deal with inequitable behaviour (eg being able to suspend or expel participants for unacceptable behaviour). Establish a code of conduct that is part of the conditions of membership to your club or team. This could include things such as:
  - treating each other with respect
  - not using racist or sexist language
  - praising effort
  - not bullying or ridiculing other participants
  - acting sensitively with regard to the feelings of others.
- Avoid confrontation.
- Select the most appropriate time and place to challenge inequitable behaviour (eg discreetly during breaks or directly in front of the rest of the group).
- Act as you would want participants to act (ie be a good role model).
- Use language that is relevant, sensitive and appropriate.
- Devise a way to punish persistent offenders (eg suspend or fine players who break the code of conduct).
- Devise a way to reward fair play and equitable behaviour.
- Point out that just because a team member doesn't appear to mind being referred to in an inequitable way, not everyone else will put up with it.

The next activity takes the examples of inequitable behaviour from Activity 6 and asks you to think about how you would deal with them.

ACTIVITY 7

Re-read the following examples of inequitable behaviour and make a note of how you would deal with them in the right-hand column. Don't worry if you find this difficult – some suggestions are provided on page 71.

Scenario	How to Deal With It
1 You are coaching a group of men and you hear one player telling the rest of the team that they are useless and playing like a bunch of girls.	
2 You find out that one of the children you coach has received a note signed by other team members telling her she's no longer wanted on the team because she's too fat.	
3 You coach both men and women at your club. You notice that every time you coach two of the younger women, several of the men watch and make comments about the way they are dressed and other suggestive comments, which the women obviously find upsetting.	

Scenario	How to Deal With It
4 You are told that some lesbian participants who attend your coaching sessions are frequently heard telling some of the young girls at the club that men are 'no good' and that they 'can't be trusted'.	
5 Several of your club's members are from ethnic minorities. One day, one of these members draws your attention to a poster on the coaching notice board, which has been defaced with racist graffiti. You are given the names of the perpetrators, one of whom is a star player at the club.	
6 After a training session, you enter a changing room to see several young participants taunting another participant who wears glasses. One person even takes his glasses from him and stands on them.	
7 You hear one of your participants telling another participant that he is playing 'like a spastic'.	

Now turn over.

Supersport Photographs

Feedback

The table below contains suggested ways of dealing with the examples of inequitable behaviour in Activity 7. These are by no means the only methods – you may well have come up with others that would be more appropriate for your coaching situation.

Scenario	How to Deal With It
1 *You are coaching a group of men and you hear one player telling the rest of the team that they are useless and playing like a bunch of girls.*	• *Take the participant to one side and suggest that this is not an appropriate way to talk because it implies that women are not as good at sport as men. It is also not positive to tell a group they are useless. Remind the participant of the club's code of conduct.* • *Alternatively, talk to the whole group and ask them how they felt about being spoken to in that way and, more importantly, how they think women would have felt if they had overheard what was said.*
2 *You find out that one of the children you coach has received a note signed by other team members telling her she's no longer wanted on the team because she's too fat.*	• *Speak to the team as a whole (and their parents or carers if relevant) and tell them you have found out that some unfair behaviour has been going on, which has upset one team member in particular. Say how disappointed you are with their behaviour and that, unless it stops, you may have to take further action (eg cancelling a tournament or trip to see a professional game).* • *Speak to the child who received the note (and perhaps a parent or carer). Make it clear that you support them and try to boost their self-esteem.*
3 *You coach both men and women at your club. You notice that every time you coach two of the younger women, several of the men watch and make comments about the way they are dressed and other suggestive comments, which the women obviously find upsetting.*	• *Speak to the men and point out that they are breaking the club's code of conduct and upsetting the women involved.* • *If the men continue to behave inequitably, you could exclude or suspend them (if this is allowed under your club constitution or code of conduct).*

Scenario	How to Deal With It
4 *You are told that some lesbian participants who attend your coaching sessions are frequently heard telling some of the young girls at the club that men are 'no good' and that they 'can't be trusted'.*	• *Talk to the women and ask them to keep their opinions to themselves. Point out that their language is homophobic and not acceptable.* • *Remind them of the club's code of conduct and ask them to try to act in a positive way by supporting the male club members.*
5 *Several of your club's members are from ethnic minorities. One day, one of these members draws your attention to a poster on the coaching notice board, which has been defaced with racist graffiti. You are given the names of the perpetrators, one of whom is a star player at the club.*	• *Establish whether or not the names you have been given are correct.* • *Talk to the participants involved and point out that their actions are racist and will not be tolerated at the club. You could also tell them that they could be suspended or thrown out of the club because of their behaviour (if this is allowed under your club constitution or code of conduct).* • *The fact that one of the perpetrators is a star player should not affect the way you act, unless you use it to emphasise that he is a role model for other club members and should therefore act equitably.* • *Ask the perpetrators to post a written apology on the notice board and to make a verbal apology to the club members from ethnic minorities.* • *If you are unable to establish who the perpetrators are, speak to the club as a whole, highlighting the club's code of conduct and the action that could be taken against those who go against it. You could also put up posters reminding players of their responsibility to act in an equitable way towards each other.*

The information in this section is by no means exhaustive, nor a definitive guide. It is intended to provide general guidance only and is not a substitute for professional legal advice.

Section Six

Legal Framework Affecting Equity

6.0 What's In It For You?

Providing sporting opportunities for everyone in society regardless of their ability, race and gender is not just a moral responsibility, but could also be a legal requirement in some instances, particularly for organisations deemed to be *service providers* (eg local authorities, national governing bodies, sporting organisations).

By delivering coaching sessions, you are providing a service, but this does not necessarily classify you as the service provider in the eyes of the law. If you are employed by another party (eg sports club), your employer is ultimately responsible for your actions. More often than not, it is the employ*er*, not the employ*ee*, who is cited in employment tribunal/court cases. However, this should not be used as an excuse for inequitable practice on your part. You still have an important role to play in helping your employer respond to equity legislation and other equity-related initiatives. You may find yourself being asked to ensure that, where possible, your coaching sessions are open and accessible to all sections of the community.

On the other hand, you may be one of the many coaches who work on a voluntary basis in a wide variety of situations and who receive little or no payment for their services and expertise, and little advice and support. Although the service you provide may not be subject to the same legal requirements as that of official *service providers*, it is still essential that your coaching sessions are as equitable as possible and that they reflect best practice at all times.

Whether you are an employed or voluntary coach, it is important that you are aware of the legal framework that affects equity. This section will introduce you to three sources of liability with which all coaches should be familiar:

- Discrimination (Section 6.1)
- Negligence (Section 6.2)
- Defamation (Section 6.3).

6.1 Discrimination

What is Discrimination?

Discrimination is the action people take on the basis of their prejudices. It occurs when a prejudiced person has the power to put their prejudices into action, which results in unfair and unjust treatment. There are two types of discrimination:

- **Direct discrimination** occurs when someone is treated worse than other people in the same or similar situation.
- **Indirect discrimination** occurs when there is a rule or condition that applies to everybody, but people from a certain group are not able to meet it and there is no justifiable reason for having that rule.

This section provides a brief overview of the key discrimination-related legislation you need to be aware of:

- Disability Discrimination Act 1995
- Race Relations Act 1976 and Race Relations (Amendment) Act 2000
- Race Relations (Northern Ireland) Order 1997
- Sex Discrimination Act 1975
- Northern Ireland Act 1998
- Scotland Act 1998.

The aim of the section is to help you understand how these key Acts could affect coaching practice.

Disability Discrimination Act 1995

The Disability Discrimination Act 1995 applies to England, Northern Ireland, Scotland and Wales. Part III of the Disability Discrimination Act 1995 makes it unlawful for people who provide goods, facilities or services to the public to discriminate against disabled people. The Act calls these people *service providers.*

Service providers must treat disabled people in the same way they would treat other people when offering a service or facility, whether for payment or not. In addition, they must make all reasonable adjustments to the environment in which they operate to accommodate an individual's impairment. This involves:

- changing any policies, practices and procedures that might discriminate against disabled people
- providing auxiliary aids and services
- providing their services by a reasonable alternative means if there is a physical barrier to access.

In 2004, the final stage for implementing Part III of the Act will be introduced. Service providers will be required to change or avoid physical features that prevent disabled people using their service.

Discrimination occurs when a disabled person is treated less favourably than someone else and this treatment:

- is for a reason relating to the person's disability and that reason does not apply to the other person
- cannot be justified.

Unlawful discrimination occurs when a service provider discriminates by:

- refusing to serve a disabled person
- offering a disabled person a lower standard of service
- offering a disabled person less favourable terms
- failing to make alterations to a service or facility, which makes it impossible or unreasonably difficult for a disabled person to use.

Abuse and harassment (eg insensitive language, persistent remarks) are forms of disability discrimination.

Action Plus

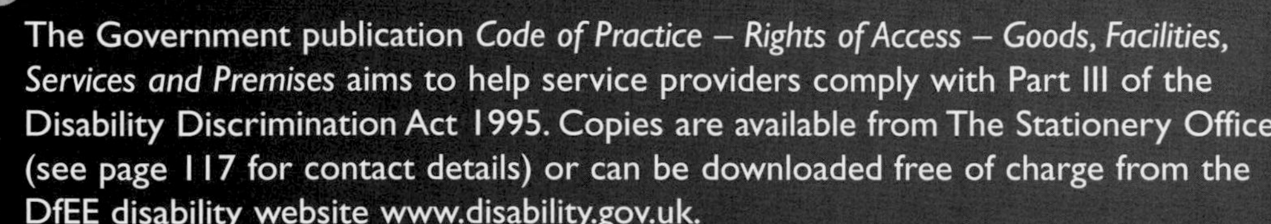

- The Government publication *Code of Practice – Rights of Access – Goods, Facilities, Services and Premises* aims to help service providers comply with Part III of the Disability Discrimination Act 1995. Copies are available from The Stationery Office (see page 117 for contact details) or can be downloaded free of charge from the DfEE disability website www.disability.gov.uk.
- Appendix D contains some useful suggestions on providing services to disabled people. Although not specifically aimed at coaches, you will nonetheless find them useful.
- For further information on the Disability Discrimination Act 1995 and related issues, contact the Disability Rights Commission (see page 112 for contact details).

Implications for You

At present in the UK, there are very few examples of legal proceedings that have been brought against coaches under the Disability Discrimination Act 1995. However, this is not to say it couldn't happen.

In order to promote best practice when deciding whether to involve disabled people in your coaching sessions, you should:

- always assess participants on the basis of their ability, ***not*** disability
- have an open mind and no preconceived ideas of what level of performance you think a particular participant is at
- advertise your coaching sessions in the right places (ie places that disabled people attend)
- find out if your national governing body has any recommendations on how to incorporate disabled people into your coaching sessions
- establish if you would need specialist equipment
- find out about workshops/courses you could attend to improve your knowledge of coaching disabled people – for example:

sports coach UK workshops:

- How to Coach Disabled People in Sport (Coaching Essentials Workshop)
- Coaching Disabled Performers (Develop Your Coaching Workshop)

Workshop dates and locations are available from the Business Support Centre.

See page 111 for contact details.

National governing body sport-specific courses

Many national governing bodies run courses designed to assist those working with disabled sportspeople. Find out what your national governing body has to offer.

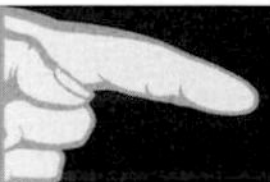

These are just some of the things to bear in mind when coaching disabled people – refer back to Section Four for further guidance.

The following organisations can offer further advice and support on working with disabled people:

- Disability Rights Commission
- Disability Sport Cymru
- Disability Sports NI (DSNI)
- English Federation of Disability Sport (EFDS)
- Local disability rights organisation (if one is available)
- Local authority
- Royal National Institute for the Blind (RNIB)
- Scottish Disability Sport.

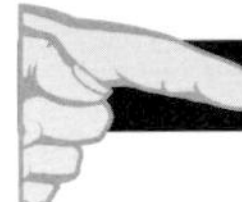

See pages 112 to 113 for contact details.

Race Relations Act 1976

The Race Relations Act 1976 applies to England, Scotland and Wales, but not Northern Ireland (see page 80 for Northern Ireland equivalent). It gives anyone who thinks they may have been discriminated against on racial grounds (ie because of their race, colour, nationality or ethnic or national origin), the right to seek justice in the courts or employment tribunals. It covers the following areas:

- education
- employment
- housing
- provision of goods, facilities and services
- training.

The Act deals with people's discriminatory actions and the effect of their actions. Motives do not matter, but if someone's attitude is proven to be racist, as well as their actions being discriminatory, this will count against them in any court tribunal.

Racist abuse and harassment (eg insensitive language, persistent remarks) are forms of racial discrimination.

Note

Incidents in public places, such as racial abuse in the street or at a football match, are not covered by the Race Relations Act. These are dealt with under the Public Order Act and the Football Offences Act respectively.

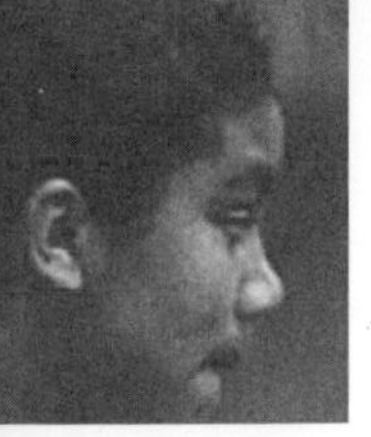

Race Relations (Amendment) Act 2000

The Race Relations (Amendment) Act 2000[1] is the first major reform of the Race Relations Act 1976 and aims to provide wider protection against racial discrimination. The Act amends the 1976 Act in two main ways:

- It makes it unlawful for any public authority, in relation to any of its activities, to discriminate on racial grounds whether directly, indirectly or by victimisation[1]. This applies not only to statutory bodies (eg local authorities), but also to any private or voluntary body when carrying out public functions.
- It makes it a duty for all public authorities to have due regard to the need to eliminate racial discrimination and to promote racial equality.

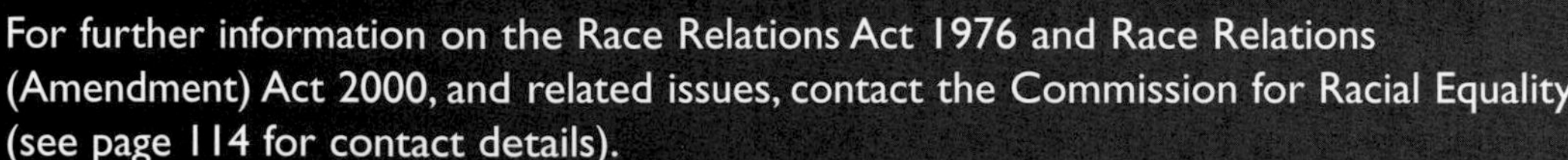

For further information on the Race Relations Act 1976 and Race Relations (Amendment) Act 2000, and related issues, contact the Commission for Racial Equality (see page 114 for contact details).

Race Relations (Northern Ireland) Order 1997

The Race Relations (Northern Ireland) Order is based on the Race Relations Act 1976 and became law in 1997. Section 21 of the Act makes it unlawful for people who provide goods, facilities or services to the public, or a section of the public, to discriminate on racial grounds against people seeking to obtain or use those goods, facilities or services by:

- refusing or deliberately omitting to provide them with goods, facilities or services, or
- refusing or deliberately omitting to provide them with goods, facilities or services of the same quality, in the same manner and on the same terms as other members of the public.

Section 38 of the Act relates specifically to sports and competitions. It outlines circumstances when discrimination on the basis of nationality or place of birth, or the length of time somebody has been resident in a particular area or place, is acceptable. This is only when:

- selecting one or more persons to represent a country, place or area, or any related association, in any sport or game, or
- abiding by the rules of any competition so far as they relate to eligibility to compete in any sport or game.

1 See the *racial discrimination* entry in Appendix A for definitions of these terms.

For further information on the Race Relations (Northern Ireland) Order 1997 and related issues, contact the Equality Commission for Northern Ireland (see page 115 for contact details).

Implications for You

At present in the UK, there are very few examples of legal proceedings that have been brought against coaches under the Race Relations Act 1976 or Race Relations (Northern Ireland) Act 1997. However, this is not to say it couldn't happen. The panel below shows examples of action taken against racial discrimination in rugby league and football.

Rugby League

In October 2000, an employment tribunal found Leeds Rhinos Rugby Super League Club guilty of 'unconscious racial discrimination'. It ruled that a black player was discriminated against when the head coach told him he would not get a first team place 'irrespective of performance'. The head coach's comments were deemed 'ill-considered' and the club was accused of failing to adequately investigate the allegations of racial discrimination made by the player against the head coach.

Football

Although not as widespread as it was during the 1970s and 1980s, the problem of racism in football still exists. To help combat this, football authorities have begun to fine individual clubs for racial abuse administered by their fans towards players from ethnic minorities of opposing clubs (eg UEFA fined Red Star Belgrade £16,000 for the racist behaviour of its fans towards black players in the Leicester City team during a Champions League match in 2000). Rather than bringing charges of racial discrimination against individuals, football clubs are now held responsible for the behaviour of their fans.

In 2000, The Football Association (The FA) introduced a new set of disciplinary guidelines designed to clean up the image of English football. Within these, it specifies that clubs are responsible for crowd control and face fines or point deductions if fans behave in an unacceptable manner. In addition, any offence motivated by discrimination on racial grounds will result in double the usual penalty.

In order to promote best practice when working with participants from ethnic minorities, you should:

- always assess participants on the basis of their ability, ***not*** race
- have an open mind and no preconceived ideas about people from ethnic minorities, and always treat everyone fairly
- always use language that is sensitive, appropriate and relevant
- ensure that all participants behave appropriately during your coaching sessions and do not offend others.

These are just some of things to bear in mind when coaching people from ethnic minorities – refer back to Section Four for further guidance.

The following organisations can offer further advice and support on working with people from ethnic minorities:

- Commission for Racial Equality
- Equal Opportunities Commission
- Equality Commission for Northern Ireland
- Sporting Equals.

See pages 114 to 115 for contact details.

sports coach UK

Sex Discrimination Act 1975

The Sex Discrimination Act 1975 applies to England, Northern Ireland, Scotland and Wales. The underlying principle of the Sex Discrimination Act 1975 is that men and women should be treated equally. Section 29 of the Act requires equality in the provision of goods, facilities and services to the public or a section of the public, whether for payment or not.

When passing the Act, however, Parliament decided there should be exceptions to the general rule of equal treatment in special circumstances. The sections of the Act that are particularly relevant to the sport and leisure industry are summarised below:

- Section 35 (1) c) allows facilities or services to be restricted to one sex if it can be demonstrated that they are such that users of one sex are:
  - more likely to suffer serious embarrassment at the presence of the opposite sex, or
  - likely to be in a state of undress and might reasonably object to the presence of users of the opposite sex.
- Section 35 (2) permits single sex provision if physical contact is likely between users of the opposite sex and there might be a reasonable objection to this.
- Section 34 permits voluntary groups of various kinds to cater for one sex only. Such organisations may restrict membership, benefits and facilities to one sex and may provide public services to one sex only.

Sexual harassment is a form of sexual discrimination. It is unwanted, often sexual attention and may include:

- written or verbal abuse or threats
- sexually-oriented comments
- jokes, lewd comments or sexual innuendos
- taunts about body, dress, marital status or sexuality
- shouting and/or bullying
- ridiculing or undermining of performance or self-respect
- sexual or homophobic graffiti
- practical jokes based on sex
- intimidating sexual remarks, invitations or familiarity
- domination of meetings, training sessions or equipment
- condescending or patronising behaviour
- physical contact, fondling, pinching or kissing
- sex-related vandalism
- offensive telephone calls or photos
- bullying on the basis of sex.

Text reproduced with the kind permission of WomenSport International from their leaflet ***Sexual Harassment and Abuse in Sport.*** *See page 115 for contact details.*

For further information on the Sex Discrimination Act 1975 and related issues, contact the Equal Opportunities Commission (see page 115 for contact details).

Implications for You

At present in the UK, there are very few examples of legal proceedings that have been brought against coaches under the Sex Discrimination Act 1975. However, this is not to say it couldn't happen. The panel below shows an example of action taken against sex discrimination in football.

Hardwick v The Football Association

In 1997, Vanessa Hardwick successfully claimed that The FA sexually discriminated against her on a two-week coaching course. Her case was backed by the Equal Opportunities Commission. She complained that the course had been dominated by men, that she had been deliberately left out of certain role plays and that, despite achieving better marks than a number of men who had passed an earlier course, she was failed.

The tribunal decided that The FA had deliberately failed her on the grounds that she was a woman and she was awarded £5000 for injury to feelings. The tribunal requested that she be awarded the coaching qualification or receive further damages.

Two years later, the tribunal ruled that Hardwick should receive £16,000 compensation for potential loss of earnings and recommended that she be awarded her Advanced Coaching Licence within 28 days.

In order to promote best practice when working with mixed gender groups, you should:

- always assess participants on the basis of their ability, ***not*** gender
- have an open mind and no preconceived ideas about women's and girls' abilities, and always treat everyone fairly
- try to develop team selection criteria based on ability and always be able to provide written comments to justify your decision to select particular participants
- try to involve team captains or others when selecting teams to avoid any biased decisions
- use language which is sensitive, appropriate and relevant
- ensure appropriate facilities are available to accommodate all participants' needs.

These are just some of the things to bear in mind when coaching women and girls – refer back to Section Four for further guidance.

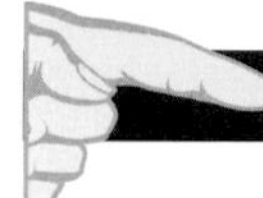

The following organisations can offer further advice and support on working with women and girls:

- Equality Commission for Northern Ireland
- Equal Opportunities Commission
- Women's Sports Foundation.

See page 115 for contact details.

Northern Ireland Act 1998

Section 75 of the Northern Ireland Act 1998 states that, when carrying out their functions, all public bodies[1] must have due regard to the need to promote equality of opportunity between:

- persons of different religious belief, political opinion, racial group, age, marital status or sexual orientation
- men and women generally
- persons with a disability and persons without
- persons with dependants and persons without.

In addition, public bodies must promote good relations between people of different religious belief, political opinion or racial group, underpinned by three principles – equity, respecting diversity and interdependence.

In order to comply with Section 75 of the Northern Ireland Act 1998, all public bodies have been required to produce an Equality Scheme. This must highlight all their policies (both written and unwritten), procedures and practices. It must also include timescales by which all policies will be reviewed to ensure that everyone, regardless of their category, has equal access to their services.

1 Public bodies are organisations such as district councils, health trusts, education and library boards and non-departmental government agencies such as the Sports Council for Northern Ireland, Arts Council, Probation Board for Northern Ireland and Water Service.

Scotland Act 1998

The Scotland Act 1998 gives the Scottish Parliament powers to promote equal opportunities for a broad range of groups and to encourage others to do so as well. The Act defines *equal opportunities* as:

> *... the prevention, elimination or regulation of discrimination between persons on grounds of sex or marital status, on racial grounds, or on grounds of disability, age, sexual orientation, language or social origin, or of other personal attributes, including beliefs or options, such as religious beliefs or political opinions.*
>
> ***Scotland Act 1998***

The Scottish Executive has recognised that, while many communities live and work in harmony, some experience harassment, discrimination and exclusion. November 2000 saw the launch of its equality strategy *Working Towards Equality.* Through this strategy, the Scottish Executive aims to work with people and organisations to:

- remove the causes of discrimination and prejudice
- strengthen and build on what is positive and inclusive
- promote a fair and just Scotland where:
  - everyone has the opportunity to fulfil their potential in all areas of life
  - no-one is excluded
  - people respect each other and their differences.

Supersport Photographs

Did You Know ...?

Disability Discrimination Act 1995

1 The Disability Discrimination Act 1995 covers people:
- with **physical impairments**
- with **learning disabilities**
- whose **mental health is impaired**
- who **use hearing aids**

  ... but **not** people who **wear glasses.**

2 It is **lawful** to provide separate coaching sessions for disabled people, but unlawful to provide separate sessions for non-disabled people.

3 All sports facilities are **legally required** to provide auxiliary aids to enable disabled people to use them. In **2004**, they will also be **legally required** to make their premises accessible to disabled people.

Race Relations Act 1976

1 When selecting a team or rules relating to eligibility to compete in a sport or game, it is sometimes **lawful** to discriminate on the basis of:
- nationality
- place of birth
- length of time lived in a particular area

... but **unlawful** to discriminate on the basis of:
- race or ethnic origin
- colour.

2 It is **lawful** to discriminate in the provision of separate training courses for sports staff (eg training for black people in leisure management).

3 It is **unlawful** for ethnic groups to set up their own sporting organisations and exclude people on the grounds of ethnic origin or national group.

Sex Discrimination Act 1975

1 In some circumstances, it is **lawful** to provide and advertise single-gender sports facilities.

2 It is **unlawful** to staff a women-only sports session with a male coach.

Based on information from Nottingham University (1999) ***Equality in sport means quality sport***. National Sports Development Seminar Facilitator's Pack

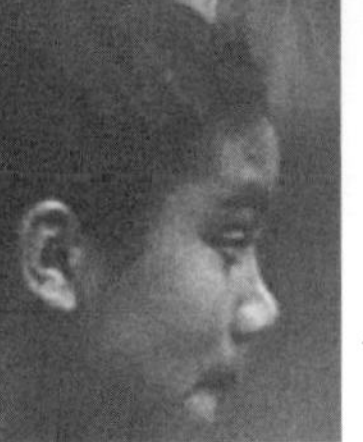

6.2 Negligence

By far the most serious of the sources of liability explored in this pack would be a claim that a participant under your supervision had suffered injury, loss or damage because of your negligence as a coach. This section highlights the need for you to be aware of action that may be required of you during coaching sessions to avoid instances of injury, loss or damage occurring, particularly when coaching disabled people.

There are four elements that together constitute a case for negligence:

- There exists a *duty of care*[1] towards the participant.
- This duty of care imposes a standard and negligence has caused that standard to be breached.
- The participant has suffered loss, harm, damage or injury.
- The breach of duty contributes to the loss, harm, damage or injury.

sports coach UK

1 See pages 89 to 90 for further information about duty of care.

Duty of Care

As a coach, you have a duty to be:

Safe

- In any coaching environment where there is a forseeable risk of harm (this includes indoors, outdoors, wet and dry), you must carry out a risk assessment of the activity to be carried out within that environment and be able to provide documentary evidence to support that assessment.
- No-one can completely eliminate the risk of harm, but you must show evidence of having acted reasonably to minimise risks as far as humanly possible (eg safety of venue, equipment and playing surfaces).
- Make your participants fully aware of the risks involved in particular activities. This needs to be done repeatedly, clearly and thoroughly. Remember that a novice may not necessarily have the same comprehension or appreciation of the risks as an intermediate or expert participant.
- It is important to plan and deliver appropriate coaching sessions to meet the needs of your participants. This means selecting appropriate activities for the age, physical and emotional maturity, experience and ability of participants.
- Ensure participants are made aware of the health and safety guidelines, which operate in your sport environment and within your governing body of sport.
- Reinforce and, if possible, practice emergency procedures.
- Encourage *fair play* and penalise incidences of *foul play* in your sport.
- Ensure participants stick to the rules and take as few risks as possible on their way to achieving their goals.

The **sports coach UK** Coaching Essentials Workshop and Study Pack *How to Coach Sports Safely* provide further information on ensuring the safety of your participants. Workshop dates and locations are available from the Business Support Centre.

See page 111 for contact details.

Qualified:

- To ensure your coaching is in line with the recommended good practice advocated by your national governing body and **sports coach UK**, you should obtain coaching qualifications. National governing bodies can provide sport-specific training, while **sports coach UK** workshops and resources[1] provide general support and guidance that underpin coach education courses.
- Your coaching qualifications should be:
  - relevant
  - at the appropriate level
  - current and up to date.

1 Further details available from **Coachwise 1st4sport** (see page 111 for contact details).

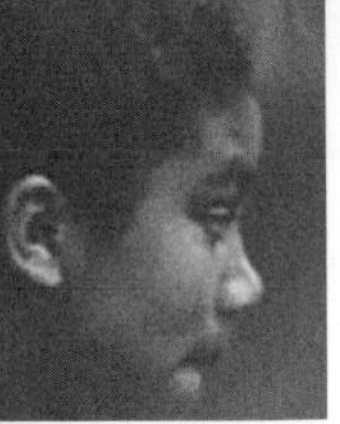

Competent

- You should only coach those elements of your sport for which your training and competence is recognised by your national governing body.
- The National Occupational Standards for Coaching, Teaching and Instructing (and/or approved national governing body coaching awards) provide the framework for assessing competence at the different levels of coaching practice. Competence to coach should normally be verified through evidence of qualifications. Competence cannot be inferred solely from evidence of prior experience.
- You must be able to recognise and accept when to refer participants to other coaches or agencies. It is your responsibility, as far as possible, to verify the competence and integrity of any other person to whom you refer a participant.
- You should regularly seek ways of increasing your personal and professional development.
- You should welcome evaluation of your work by colleagues and be able to account to participants, employers, NGBs and colleagues for what you do and why.
- You have a responsibility to yourself and your participants to maintain your own effectiveness, resilience and abilities. You should recognise when your personal resources are so depleted that help is needed. This may necessitate the withdrawal from coaching temporarily or permanently.

Insured

- Insurance is essential for coaches, participants and sports providers (eg coaches, local authorities, governing bodies).
- Some national governing bodies do not allow coaches or participants to take part in their sport without insurance cover, while others include insurance as part of their affiliation fee. Check if your governing body operates an insurance scheme.
- **sports coach UK** Membership Services[1] provides qualified coaches with insurance as part of its benefits package.
- Insurance should cover both public liability and personal accidents, and must be adequate for the risks faced in the particular sport.

Further information on the responsibilities of coaches is available in:

- **sports coach UK** *Code of Practice for Sports Coaches*[2]
- National Occupational Standards for Coaching, Teaching and Instructing[3] – Section 7.3: Values Statement and Code of Ethics for Coaching, Teaching and Instructing.

1 and 2 Available from **Coachwise 1st4sport** (see page 111 for contact details).
3 Available from SPRITO (see page 117 for contact details).

Negligence can be attributed both to your *actions* as well as your *omissions*. Injured participants have the right to sue coaches who may have caused injury by negligence. To do so, they would have to prove it was a breach of the standards demanded by the duty of care that caused loss or injury. This is described as the *but for* test:

But for the actions of the coach, would the loss or injury have occurred?

The following case study is an example of a court case brought by a disabled archer. It illustrates the duty of care you owe your participants.

Morrell v Owen and Others

In 1993, Mr Justice Mitchell adjudged that organisers and coaches of sporting activities owe a greater duty of care to disabled people than they would to non-disabled people.

The incident that brought about this judgement occurred during a training session held in 1993 by the British Amputee and Les Autres Sports Association (BALASA) in a sports hall in Birmingham. Two activities, archery and discus, were in progress in the same sports hall, which was divided by a fishnet curtain.

Miss Morrell, a disabled archer, was injured by a discus that struck the dividing curtain and hit her on the side of the head. The coaches present claimed they had warned Miss Morrell of the dangers of the activity at the other side of the curtain. Miss Morrell, however, claimed that she had not been warned. Mr Justice Mitchell believed Miss Morrell, stating that the kind of misthrow that occurred was entirely foreseeable, as was the accident in question. He stated that the coaches present owed a greater duty of care to the disabled people than they would to non-disabled people.

Implications for You

The *Morrell v Owen and Others* case illustrates how important it is for you to ensure that, when coaching disabled people, you take all the necessary measures to ensure your sessions are as safe as possible. You are strongly recommended to attend workshops/courses to improve your knowledge of coaching disabled people – for example:

sports coach UK workshops:

- How to Coach Disabled People in Sport (Coaching Essentials Workshop)
- Coaching Disabled Performers (Develop Your Coaching Workshop)

Workshop dates and locations are available from the Business Support Centre.

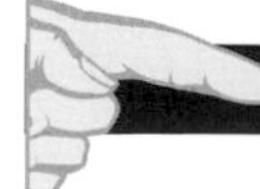

See page 111 for contact details.

National governing body sport-specific courses

Many national governing bodies run courses designed to assist those working with disabled sportspeople. Find out what your national governing body has to offer.

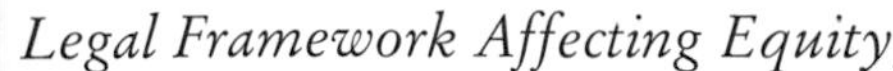

6.3 Defamation

Defamation is a statement that injures the reputation of another by exposing them to hatred, contempt or ridicule, or that tends to lower them in the esteem of right-thinking members of society.

There are two types of defamation:

- Slander – the spoken word
- Libel – the written word.

The following story illustrates defamation and describes a situation that could occur in any sports club at any level.

> Alison is a coach at a local athletics club. She successfully applies to become part of the coaching team responsible for the elite squad at the club. Tushar is an up-and-coming member of the elite squad with potential to do well at the next regional athletics meeting. He is one of five athletes that Alison has specific responsibility for. However, Tushar finds it difficult to get on with Alison. She is always making derogatory remarks about him and purposefully ignores him during group coaching sessions, devoting more time to the other athletes. Tushar's performance consequently suffers and he misses out on a place in the club team.
>
> Disappointed, Tushar asks to be moved to a different group with a different coach. Alison says that Tushar's poor form has nothing to do with her and that he should be more committed to his training if he wants to do well.
>
> Tushar moves to a different group and is much happier. His performance improves dramatically and he comfortably wins the 100m final at the next regional athletics meeting. After the race, Alison is overheard telling her group of athletes that Tushar is selfish and attention-seeking. She adds that she doesn't know how Tushar managed to do so well and that he must have taken performance-enhancing drugs to have made such a dramatic improvement in such a short space of time.

In the example above, Alison acted in an inappropriate and unprofessional manner, and could well have lost her position as coach at the athletics club. Make sure you never put yourself in a position where this could happen to you. Always set an example to your participants in terms of behaviour and attitude. Your professional relationship and attitude towards officials, spectators and other coaches must also be of the highest standard. Think about the influence your behaviour will have on your participants, parents and other coaches. Try to be consistent and fair in what you say, what you do and what you ask of others.

6.4 Summary

This section should have helped you to understand the legal framework that affects equity. The key points you need to remember are listed in the panel opposite.

DISCRIMINATION

- Discrimination is the action people take on the basis of their prejudices. It occurs when a prejudiced person has the power to put their prejudices into action, which results in unfair and unjust treatment. There are two types of discrimination – direct and indirect.
- Key discrimination-related legislation includes:
  - Disability Discrimination Act 1995
  - Race Relations Act 1976 and Race Relations (Amendment) Act 2000
  - Race Relations (Northern Ireland) Order 1997
  - Sex Discrimination Act 1975
  - Northern Ireland Act 1998
  - Scotland Act 1998.
- To avoid allegations of discrimination being made against you or your employer, always promote best practice when working with the key target groups.

NEGLIGENCE

- All coaches have a duty to be:
  - safe
  - qualified
  - competent
  - insured.

  This is known as *duty of care*.
- Negligence on the part of the coach causes a breach of duty and can result in a participant suffering injury, loss or damage.
- To avoid allegations of negligence being made against you, ensure you are aware of action that may be required of you during coaching sessions, particularly when coaching disabled people. Remember, negligence can be attributed both to your actions as well as your omissions.

DEFAMATION

- Defamation is a statement that injures the reputation of another by exposing them to hatred, contempt or ridicule, or that tends to lower them in the esteem of right-thinking members of society.
- There are two types of defamation:
  - Slander – the spoken word
  - Libel – the written word.
- To avoid allegations of defamation being made against you, always set an example to your participants in terms of behaviour and attitude.

Action Plus

Section Seven

Action Plan for Change

7.0 What's In It For You?

By now, you should appreciate just how vital it is to ensure that your coaching practice is as equitable as possible. But however inspired you may feel to make improvements in the necessary areas, putting the theory into practice may seem rather daunting. Where do you start? To what extent should you aim to attract the key target groups to your coaching sessions?

By the end of this section you should be able to:

- identify areas you feel need improving or developing in your coaching practice
- explain why developing an equity policy is a good idea
- develop an action plan for adopting equity principles into your coaching practice.

7.1 Identifying Areas for Change

Before you can plan for change, you need to identify the areas you feel need improving or developing. The following ideas should help you do this:

- Use national population statistics as a general guide to gauge how equitable your coaching sessions are. However, remember that they only reflect the national average and that you also need to bear in mind the huge regional/local variations that can occur.

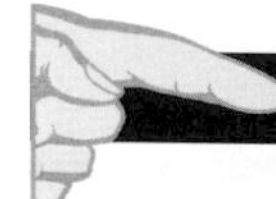
See pages 6 to 8 for further details.

- Ask another coach to observe one of your coaching sessions with particular reference to equity issues (eg the language you use). Compare their feedback with your own analysis of your coaching practice.
- Talk to your participants and find out whether anything you have said or done made them feel uncomfortable (you should already be doing this anyway as part of your session evaluations). Alternatively, you could devise a questionnaire for participants to fill in anonymously in their own time.

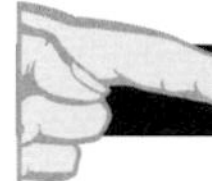
See Appendix G for a sample questionnaire.

- Find out if your national governing body has an equity policy. If so, get hold of a copy and make sure you follow its recommendations.

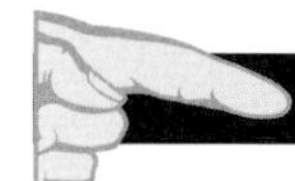
See Section 7.2 for further details about equity policies.

- Attend **sports coach UK**'s *Equity in Your Coaching* workshop and/or appropriate national governing body courses/workshops (see Section Eight for further details).
- Contact the organisations listed in Section Eight for help and advice.

7.2 Equity Statement and Policy

Assessing how equitable your coaching sessions currently are is the first stage towards ensuring they are accessible to everyone. It provides you with a starting point by which to measure your future achievements. The next stage is to demonstrate your commitment to equity.

sports coach UK has demonstrated its commitment by developing the following statement of intent:

__sports coach UK__ is committed to the principles and practices of equal opportunities, both as an employer and in the delivery of services. Employment opportunities, programmes, products and services are available to all sections of the community. __sports coach UK__ will not discriminate on the grounds of gender, marital status, race, colour, disability, sexuality, age, occupation, religion or political opinion.

sports coach UK Equity Action Plan 1999–2000

Developing a similar equity statement for your club is a good way of raising awareness, both internally and externally, of your club's commitment to providing better sporting opportunities for the key target groups. It will also help you to:

- encourage more people to participate in your sport
- encourage more people into coaching, officiating and administrating in your sport
- improve your club's public image
- show that your club is responding to equity legislation and other equity-related initiatives.

As well as developing a general equity policy, you might want to create individual policies for each of the key target groups. For example, **sports coach UK** has developed a racial equality policy.

For an equity policy to work, everybody involved in your club (eg participants, coaches, employees, volunteers) needs to recognise that their own practice is perhaps not as equitable as it should be and be prepared to do something about it. There also needs to be a commitment to implementing, monitoring and evaluating the policy, which may have implications on funding for new resources, equipment and training.

You may not personally be in a position to implement an equity policy – perhaps this would be the responsibility of club management or perhaps you are self-employed and coach at a variety of different venues. However, you still have a role to play in influencing the powers that be, as well as raising the awareness of participants, colleagues and other related groups about the importance of equity. There is also nothing to stop you developing your own personal equity policy to guide your coaching practice.

7.3 Putting the Theory into Practice

This pack may have highlighted specific areas in your own coaching practice that you feel you would like to improve or change altogether. Some things will be relatively easy to improve/change (eg being aware of the words and phrases you use). Other things may take a little longer and you may need to contact various organisations for assistance and advice. The next activity will help you focus on the improvements/changes required.

ACTIVITY 8

What improvements or changes do you need to make to your coaching practice?

1 In the left-hand column of the table below, list the things you can change immediately or in the short term.

2 In the right-hand column, list the improvements and/or changes that might take longer to sort out. Some examples have been given to start you off.

Short-term Improvements/Changes	Long-term Improvements/Changes
Things I can change immediately: • *Use appropriate language and terminology so that I don't upset or offend participants.* • *Make sure I don't stereotype people, but am open-minded.*	*Things I can change in the long term:* • *Set up a coaching programme to encourage more people from local ethnic minorities to take part in my sport.* • *Encourage my club to provide better facilities for disabled people.*

3 Now that you have identified the short- and long-term improvements/changes that need to be made to your coaching practice, try to put an equity action plan together:

a Select the three most important improvements/changes you listed in each column of the table above.

b Use the blank action plans provided on pages 99 and 100 to help you identify:

- how you intend to make each improvement/change
- the date by which you intend to do it.

4 Review your action plans regularly and record your achievements. No doubt you will think of new improvements/changes to add to your list in the future.

A blank copy of the action plans is provided in Appendix H for you to photocopy and use as and when required.

SHORT-TERM IMPROVEMENTS/CHANGES		
What?	**How?**	**When?**
1		
2		
3		

LONG-TERM IMPROVEMENTS/CHANGES

	What?	How?	When?
1			
2			
3			

7.4 Summary

You should now have identified areas for improvement in your coaching practice and started to put together an equity action plan, whether it be specifically for your own coaching or for your club in general.

Working through this pack may have raised issues for you that you have previously never considered in your coaching. Part of being a good coach is being open to new ideas and training and, to some extent, being aware that you need updating in certain areas. It is also about understanding the needs of the people you are coaching and accepting advice on how to accommodate them. Section Eight provides a comprehensive list of useful contacts, references and recommended reading.

sports coach UK

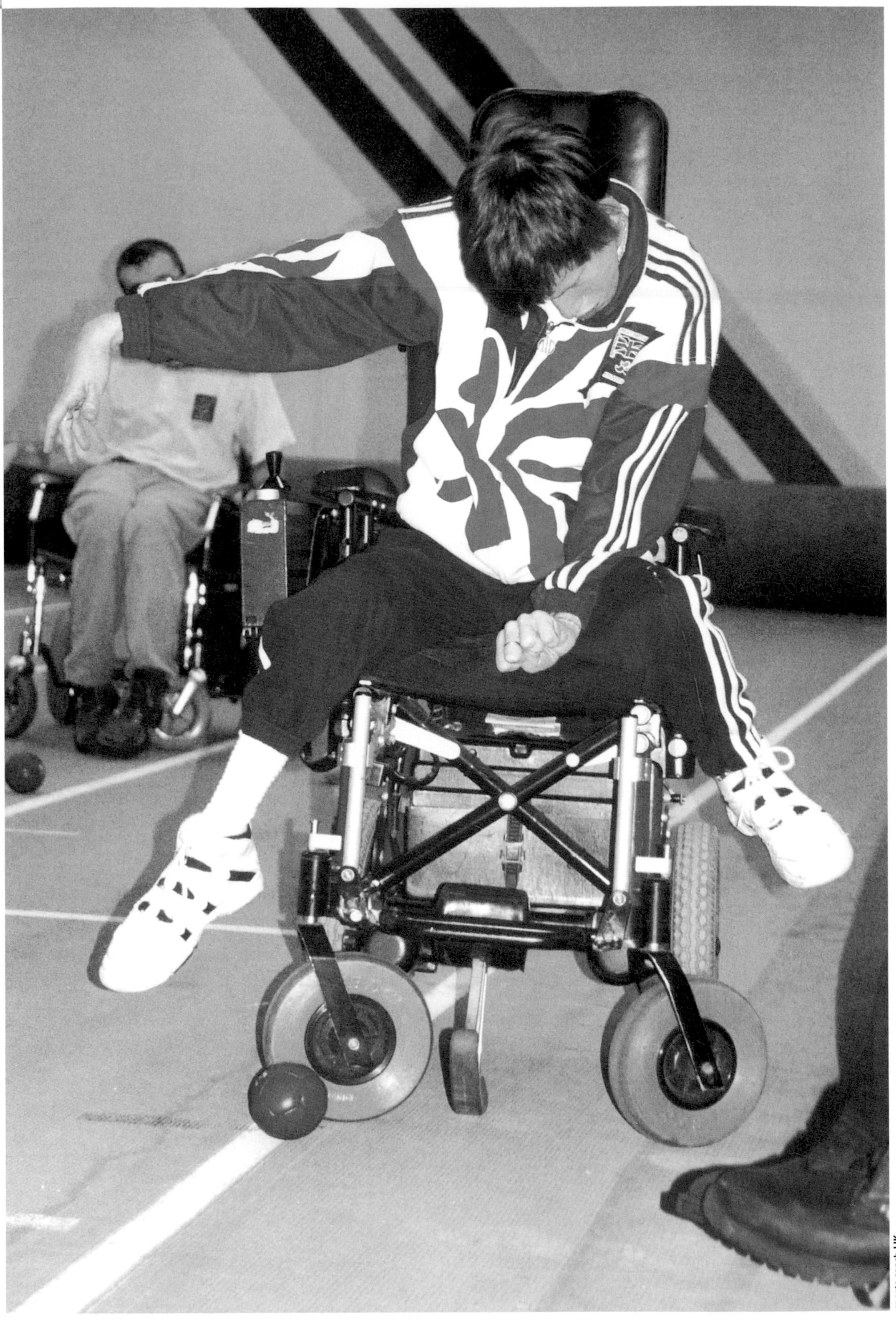

sports coach UK

Section Eight

Where Next?

8.0 Introduction

Part of being a good coach is being open to new ideas and training and, to some extent, being aware that you need updating in certain areas. It is also about understanding the needs of the people you are coaching and accepting advice on how to accommodate them. This section provides a comprehensive list of publications, workshops and organisations that can provide support and guidance on equity-related issues.

8.1 Further Reading/Workshops

This section lists a selection of useful publications and workshops that support the information provided in this pack. It is divided into subsections (one for each key target group plus a miscellaneous section) to make it easier to find the resource(s) you are looking for.

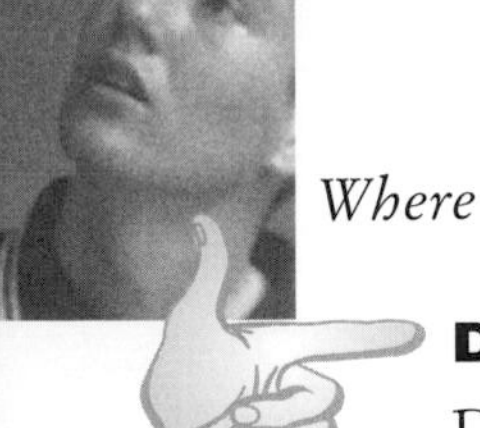

Disabled People

Disability Rights Commission (1995) ***A brief guide to the Disability Discrimination Act.*** Manchester, Disability Rights Commission. Ref no DL40

Disability Rights Commission (1996) ***The Disability Discrimination Act – definition of disability.*** Manchester, Disability Rights Commission. Ref no DL60

Disability Rights Commission (undated) ***The Disability Discrimination Act 1995 – some useful suggestions.*** Manchester, Disability Rights Commission. Ref no DL200

English Federation of Disability Sport (1999) ***Sport for disabled people.*** Alsager, English Federation of Disability Sport

English Federation of Disability Sport (2000) ***EFDS four year sports development plan for disabled people in England 2000–2004.*** Alsager, English Federation of Disability Sport

English Federation of Disability Sport (2000) ***Sport and disabled people: national governing bodies of sport – skills and coaching awards.*** Alsager, English Federation of Disability Sport

Great Britain Department of Social Security and National Disability Council (1996) ***Code of practice – rights of access – goods, facilities, services and premises.*** London, HMSO. ISBN 0 11762 432 2

Kerr, A (1998) ***Coaching disabled performers.*** Leeds, Coachwise Business Solutions/The National Coaching Foundation. ISBN 1 902523 07 5

Kerr, A and Stafford, I (2005) ***How to coach disabled people in sport.*** Leeds, Coachwise Business Solutions/The National Coaching Foundation. ISBN 1 902523 54 7

sportscotland (2000) ***Sport and people with a disability: aiming at social inclusion (research digest no 57).*** Edinburgh, **sport**scotland. ISBN 1 85060 375 8

Workshops

- *sports coach UK:*
  - How to Coach Disabled People in Sport (Coaching Essentials Workshop)
  - Coaching Disabled Performers (Develop Your Coaching Workshop)
- *English Federation of Disability Sport:*
  - Coaching Disabled Footballers
  - Including Disabled Pupils in Physical Education
- *Disability Sport England:*
  - Protecting Disabled Children and Adults in Sport and Recreation

People from Ethnic Minorities

Commission for Racial Equality (1997) ***Ethnic minority women (factsheet).*** London, Commission for Racial Equality

Commission for Racial Equality (1998) ***Education and training in Britain (factsheet).*** London, Commission for Racial Equality

Commission for Racial Equality (1998) ***Racial discrimination is against the law – campaign to increase young people's awareness of their rights under the Race Relations Act.*** London, Commission for Racial Equality

Commission for Racial Equality (1998) ***Stereotyping and racism – findings from two attitude surveys.*** London, Commission for Racial Equality

Commission for Racial Equality (1998) ***Young people in Britain (factsheet).*** London, Commission for Racial Equality

Commission for Racial Equality (1999) ***Ethnic minorities in Britain (factsheet).*** London, Commission for Racial Equality

Commission for Racial Equality (1999) ***The Stephen Lawrence enquiry – implications for racial equality.*** London, Commission for Racial Equality

Commission for Racial Equality (2000) ***Achieving racial equality: a standard for sport.*** London, Commission for Racial Equality. ISBN 1 85442 233 2

Commission for Racial Equality (undated) ***Ethnic minorities in Wales (factsheet).*** Cardiff, Commission for Racial Equality

English Cricket Board Racism Study Group (1999) ***Clean bowl racism: going forward together – a report on racial equality in cricket.*** London, English Cricket Board

English Sports Council (1997) ***Working towards racial equality in sport – a good practice guide for local authorities.*** London, English Sports Council. Ref no ESC/677R/012M/6/98

Macpherson, W (1999) ***The Stephen Lawrence inquiry: report of an inquiry by Sir William Macpherson of Cluny.*** London, The Stationery Office. Cm 4262-I

Patel, M (1999) ***Where are Britain's black coaches?*** *Faster, Higher, Stronger (FHS).* Issue Five, pp 15–16

Patel, M (2000) ***Racial equality charter for sport.*** Leeds, Sporting Equals

Rennie, N (1999) ***Tackling racism in your sport (conference notes).*** Leeds, Sporting Equals.

Rowe, N and Champion, R (2000) ***Sports participation and ethnicity in England: national survey 1999/2000 headline findings.*** London, Sport England. Ref no SE/1073

Sporting Equals (1999) ***A sporting chance – the role of sport and recreation in tackling social exclusion: tackling racism in your sport.*** National Conference of Sport and Physical Recreation Facilitator's Pack

sportscotland (2000) ***Sport and minority ethnic communities: aiming at social inclusion (research digest no 58).*** Edinburgh, **sport**scotland. ISBN 1 85060 376 6

Sports Council (1994) ***Black and ethnic minorities and sport – policy and objectives.*** London, Sports Council. Ref no SC/213/10M/6/94

Women and Girls

English Sports Council, Equal Opportunities Commission, Institute of Sport and Recreation Management and Womens Sports Foundation (1997) ***Single sex sport and leisure provision.*** London, English Sports Council, Equal Opportunities Commission, Institute of Sport and Recreation Management and Womens Sports Foundation. ISBN 1 900738 35 X

Equal Opportunities Commission (undated) ***Case decisions: goods, facilities and services.*** Manchester, Equal Opportunities Commission. ISBN 1 870358 91 0

Equal Opportunities Commission (undated) ***Sex equality and goods, facilities and services.*** Manchester, Equal Opportunities Commission. ISBN 1 870358 91 0

Equal Opportunities Commission (undated) ***The Sex Discrimination Act and Equal Pay Acts: goods, facilities and services.*** Manchester, Equal Opportunities Commission

Equal Opportunities Commission (undated) ***What the law says: goods, facilities and services.*** Manchester, Equal Opportunities Commission. ISBN 1 870358 91 0

Health Education Authority (1997) ***Active for life: promoting physical activity with young women.*** London, Health Education Authority (now Health Development Agency)

Kay, T (1994) ***Women and sport – a review of research.*** London, Sports Council

Sports Council (1993) ***Women and sport – policy and frameworks for action.*** London, Sports Council. Ref no SC/212/10M/11/93

Sports Council (1994) ***Women and sport and the challenge of change (conference report).*** London, Sports Council

Sport England (1999) ***Developing women's lives through sport and physical activity (conference report).*** London, Sport England

Sport England (1999) ***Women-friendly sports facilities: Sport England facilities fact file.*** London, Recreation Management. Ref no SE/881/9M/4/cf1

UK Sports Council and International Working Group on Women and Sport (1998) ***Women and sport – from Brighton to Windhoek: facing the challenge.*** London, UK Sports Council

WomenSport International (undated) ***Sexual harassment and abuse in sport.*** Vashon WA, WomenSport International

Women's Sports Foundation (1999) ***National action plan for women's and girls' sport and physical activity.*** London, Sport England

Women's Sports Foundation (1999) ***New millennium, new opportunities (notes from a racial equality workshop held at a Women's Sports Foundation conference)***

Women's Sports Foundation (1999) ***The key issues – a new sex equality law for Britain.*** WSF News. Spring 1999. London, Women's Sports Foundation

Women's Sports Foundation (2000) ***Women and sport information pack.*** London, Women's Sports Foundation

Women's Sports Foundation (undated) ***Sexual abuse in sport – recognition and prevention (factsheet).*** London, Women's Sports Foundation

Women's Sports Foundation (undated) ***Single sex sport and leisure provision (factsheet).*** London, Women's Sports Foundation

Workshops

- *Running Sport:*
  - GirlSport™ – Staying Active While Still Being You
- *Women's Sports Foundation:*
  - WSF Women, Get Set, Go! (a sport leadership access programme)
  - Young Elite Sportswomen's Seminars

Miscellaneous

Collins, MF, Henry IP, Houlihan, B and Buller, J (1999) ***Policy action team 10: a report to the social exclusion unit.*** London, Department for Culture, Media and Sport

Crouch, M (2005) ***Protecting children – a guide for sportspeople.*** Leeds, Coachwise Business Solutions/The National Coaching Foundation. ISBN 0 947850 50 3

Department for Culture, Media and Sport (2000) ***A sporting future for all.*** London, Department for Culture, Media and Sport. Ref no PP240

Hoey, K (2000) ***A sporting future for all – the Government's new sports strategy.*** *Faster, Higher, Stronger.* Issue Eight, pp 13–15

Institute of Sport and Recreation Management (undated) ***Best value series 14 – Sports equity.*** Melton Mowbray, Institute of Sport and Recreation Management. Ref no 193:04/00

Institute of Sport and Recreation Management (undated) ***Best value series 15 – Good practice in using sport in programmes to reduce crime and anti-social behaviour.*** Melton Mowbray, Institute of Sport and Recreation Management

Nottingham University (1999) ***Equality in sport means quality sport.*** National Sports Development Seminar Facilitator's Pack

NSPCC (2000) ***Child maltreatment in the United Kingdom: a study of the prevalence of child abuse and neglect.*** London, NSPCC

Sport England (2000) ***A club for all – welcoming all members of the community.*** Leeds, Coachwise Ltd. ISBN 1 86078 134 9

Sport England (2000) ***Making English sport inclusive: Equity guidelines for governing bodies.*** London, Sport England. Ref no SE/1043/1M/6/00

sports coach UK (2003) *How to coach sports safely.* Leeds, Coachwise Solutions/The National Coaching foundation. ISBN 1 902523 50 4

sports coach UK (2005) *Code of practice for sports coaches.* Leeds, Coachwise Business Solutions/The National Coaching Foundation.

Stevens, J (2000) ***The UK vision for coaching – a strategy into the 21st century.*** *Faster, Higher, Stronger (FHS).* Issue Eight, pp 18–20

The National Training Organisation for Sport, Recreation and Allied Occupations (1997) ***National Occupational Standards and S/NVQ guide (Level Two).*** London, SPRITO. ISBN 1 902246 04 7

The Scottish Executive Central Research Unit (2000) ***The role of sport in regenerating deprived urban areas.*** Edinburgh, The Stationery Office. Research findings no 86

The Scottish Office (1999) ***Social inclusion – opening the door to a better Scotland.*** Edinburgh, The Scottish Office

The Shap Working Party (2000) ***Shap calendar of religious festivals (August 2000 to December 2001).*** London, The Shap Working Party. ISBN 0268 2451

UK Sport (2000) ***UK vision for coaching.*** Leeds, Coachwise Ltd

Welch, M (ed) (1999) ***Towards gender equity in sports management: report of the European symposium on gender equity in the management and governance of voluntary sports organisations.*** Leeds, Leeds Metropolitan University and the Federation of Yorkshire Sport

Workshops

- *sports coach UK:*
  - Coaching and the Law
  - Equity in Your Coaching
  - Good Practice and Child Protection
- *Running Sport:*
  - A Club for All – Welcoming All Members of the Community

8.2 sports coach UK Contacts

sports coach UK
114 Cardigan Road
Headingley
Leeds LS6 3BJ
Tel: 0113-274 4802
Fax: 0113-275 5019
Email: coaching@sportscoachuk.org
Website: www.sportscoachuk.org

sports coach UK works closely with sports governing bodies and other partners to provide a comprehensive service for coaches throughout the UK. This includes an extensive programme of workshops, which have proved valuable to coaches from all types of sports and every level of experience.

For further details of **scUK** workshops in your area, contact the **scUK** Business Support Centre (BSC):

sports coach UK Business Support Centre
Sports Development Centre
Loughborough University
Loughborough
Leicestershire LE11 3TU
Tel: 01509-226130
Fax: 01509-226134
Email: bsc@sportscoachuk.org
Website: www.sportscoachuk.org/improve/workshop/search.asp

Details of all **sports coach UK** publications are available from:

Coachwise 1st4sport
Chelsea Close
Off Amberley Road
Armley
Leeds LS12 4HP
Tel: 0113-201 5555
Fax: 0113-231 9606
Email: enquiries@1st4sport.com
Website: www.1st4sport.com

8.3 Useful Contacts

This section lists a selection of organisations that can provide support and guidance on equity-related issues. It is divided into subsections (one for each key target group plus a miscellaneous section) to make it easier to find the organisation(s) you are looking for.

Disabled People

British Council of Disabled People
Litchurch Plaza
Litchurch Lane
Derby DE24 8AA
Tel: 01332-295551
Fax: 01332-295580
Email: general@bcodp.org.uk
Website: www.bcodp.org.uk

Design for Life Centre
Studio 26
Brunel University
Runnymede
Egham
Surrey TW20 0JZ
Tel: 01784-433262
Fax: 01784-470880
Email: dfl@brunel.ac.uk

Disability Information Trust
Nuffield Orthopaedic Centre
Headington
Oxford OX3 7LD
Tel: 01865-227592
Fax: 01865-227596

Disability Rights Commission
DRC Helpline
Freepost MID 02164
Stratford-upon-Avon CV37 9BR
Tel: 08457-622 633
Fax: 08457-778 878
Textphone:08457-622 644
Email: ddahelp@stra.sitel.co.uk
Website: www.drc-gb.org

Disability Scotland
Princes House
5 Shandwick Place
Edinburgh EH2 4RG
Tel: 0131-229 8632
Email: enquiries@disabilityscotland.org.uk
Website: www.disabilityscotland.org.uk

Disability Sport Cymru
National Sports Centre for Wales
Sophia Gardens
Cardiff CF1 9SW
Tel: 029-2030 0525/6
Fax: 029-2030 0599
Email: scw@scw.co.uk
Website: www.disability-sport-cymru.co.uk

Disability Sport England
Belle Vue Leisure Centre
Pink Bank Lane
Manchester M12 5GL
Tel: 0161-953 2499
Fax: 0161-953 2420
Email: info@dse.org.uk
Website: www.disabilitysport.org.uk

Disability Sports NI
Unit 10
Ormeau Business Park
8 Cromac Avenue
Belfast BT7 2JA
Tel: 028-9050 8255
Textphone: 028-9050 8254
Fax: 028-9050 8256
Email: email@dsni.co.uk
Website: www.dsni.co.uk

Disability Wales
Wernddu Court
Caerphilly Business Park
Van Road
Caerphilly CF83 3ED
Tel: 029-2088 7325
Fax: 029-2088 8702
Email: info@dwac.demon.co.uk
Website: www.dwac.demon.co.uk

Disabled Living Centres Council
Redbank House
4 St Chad's Street
Cheetham
Manchester M8 8QA
Tel: 0870-770 2866
Fax: 0870-770 2867
Textphone: 0870-770 5813
Email: dlcc@dlcc.org.uk
Website: www.dlcc.co.uk

Disabled Living Foundation
380–4 Harrow Road
London W9 2HU
Tel: 020-7289 6111
Fax: 020-7266 2922
Email: info@dlf.org.uk
Website: www.dlf.org.uk

English Federation of Disability Sport
Manchester Metropolitan University
Alsager Campus
Hassall Road
Alsager
Stoke-on-Trent ST7 2HL
Tel: 0161-247 5294
Minicom: 0161-247 5644
Fax: 0161-247 6895
Email: federation@efds.co.uk
Website: www.efds.net

Remap
Hazeldene
Seven Oaks Road
Ightham
Sevenoaks
Kent TN15 9AD
Tel: 0845-130 0456
Fax: 0845-130 0789
Email: info@remap.org.uk
Website: www.remap.org.uk

Royal Association for Disability and Rehabilitation (RADAR)
Head Office
12 City Forum
250 City Road
London EC1V 8AF
Tel: 020-7250 3222
Fax: 020-7250 0212
Email: radar@radar.org.uk
Website: www.radar.org.uk

Scottish Disability Sport
Caledonia House
South Gyle
Edinburgh EH12 9DQ
Tel: 0131-317 1130
Fax: 0131-317 1075
Email: ssadsds2@aol.com
Website: www.scottishdisabilitysport.com

People from Ethnic Minorities

BEM Sport
221 Cemetery Road
Sheffield S11 8FQ
Tel: 0114-281 9540
Fax: 0114-249 1114
Email: cumberbatch@supanet.com

Commission for Racial Equality (English HQ)
St Dunstan's House
201–11 Borough High Street
London SE1 1GZ
Tel: 020-7939 0000
Fax: 020-7939 0004
Email: info@cre.gov.uk
Website: www.cre.gov.uk

Commission for Racial Equality (Scottish HQ)
The Tun
12 Jackson's Entry
Off Holyrood Road
Edinburgh EH8 8PJ
Tel: 0131-524 2000
Fax: 0131-524 2001
Email: scotland@cre.gov.uk
Website: www.cre.gov.uk/scotland

Commission for Racial Equality (Welsh HQ)
3rd Floor
Capital Tower
Greyfriars Road
Cardiff CF1 3AG
Tel: 02920-729 200
Fax: 02920-729 220
Website: www.cre.gov.uk/wales

Kick It Out
PO Box 29544
London EC2A 4WR
Tel: 020-7684 4884
Fax: 020-7684 4885
Email: info@kickitout.org
Website: www.kickitout.org

Sporting Equals
Commision for Racial Equality
Lancaster House (3rd Floor)
67 Newhall Street
Birmingham B3 1NA
Email: sportequal@cre.gov.uk
Website:
www.cre.gov.uk/sportingequals/index

Tackle Racism in Rugby League
The British Amateur Rugby League Association
West Yorkshire House
4 New North Parade
Huddersfield HD1 5JP
Tel: 01484-544131
Fax: 01484-519985
Email: info@barla.org.uk
Website: www.barla.org.uk

The Shap Working Party
PO Box 38580
London SW1P 3XF
Tel: 020-7898 1494
Fax: 020-7898 1493
Email: mike.berry@natsoc.c-of-e.org.uk
Website:
www.support4learning.org.uk/shap/index.htm

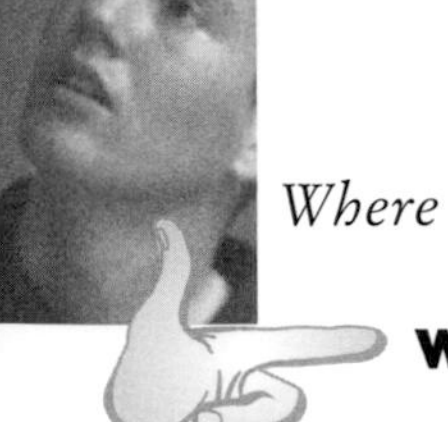

Women and Girls

WomenSport International
PO Box 743
Vashon, WA 98070
USA
Website:
www.sportsbiz.bz/womensportinternational

Women's Sports Foundation
3rd Floor, Victoria House
Bloomsbury Square
London WC1B 4SE
Tel: 020-7273 1740
Fax: 020-7273 1981
Email: info@wsf.org.uk
Website: www.wsf.org.uk

Miscellaneous

Department for Culture, Media and Sport
2–4 Cockspur Street
London SW1Y 5DH
Tel: 020-7211 6200
Email: sport@culture.gov.uk
Website: www.culture.gov.uk

Equality Commission for Northern Ireland
Equality House
7–9 Shaftesbury Square
Belfast BT2 7DP
Tel: 028-9050 0600
Textphone: 028-9050 0589
Fax: 028-9024 8687
Email: information@equalityni.org
Website: www.equalityni.org

Equal Opportunities Commission (England)
Arndale House
Arndale Centre
Manchester M4 3EQ
Tel: 0845-601 5901
Fax: 0161-838 1733
Email: info@eoc.org.uk
Website: www.eoc.org.uk

Equal Opportunities Commission (Scotland)
St Stephens House
279 Bath Street
Glasgow G2 4JL
Tel: 0845-601 5901
Fax: 0141-248 5834
Email: scotland@eoc.org.uk
Website: www.eoc.org.uk

Equal Opportunities Commission (Wales)
Windsor House
Windsor Lane
Cardiff CF10 3GE
Tel: 029-2064 1079
Fax: 029-2034 3552
Email: wales@eoc.org.uk
Website: www.eoc.org.uk

General Register Office for Scotland
Ladywell House
Ladywell Road
Edinburgh EH12 7TF
Tel: 0131-314 4254
Email: customer@gro-scotland.gov.uk
Website: www.gro-scotland.gov.uk

National Institute for Health and Clinical Excellence
MidCity Place
71 High Holborn
London WCIV 6NA
Tel: 020-7067 5800
Fax: 020-7067 5801
Website: www.nice.org.uk

Institute of Sport and Recreation Management
Sir John Beckwith Centre for Sport
Loughborough University
Loughborough LE11 3TU
Tel: 01509-226 474
Fax: 01509-226 475
Website: www.isrm.co.uk

Northern Ireland Statistics and Research Agency
McAuley House
2–14 Castle Street
Belfast BT1 1SA
Tel: 028-9034 8100
Fax: 028-9034 8106
Website: www.nisra.gov.uk

Office for National Statistics
1 Drummond Gate
London SW1V 2QQ
Tel: 020-7233 9233
Email: info@ons.gov.uk
Website: www.statistics.gov.uk

Office for National Statistics (Wales)
Cardiff Road
Newport NP10 8XG
Tel: 0845-601 3034
Fax: 01633-652 747
Email: info@statistics.gov.uk
Website: www.statistics.gov.uk

Scottish Executive
Different departments are located at different addresses – use contact details below to find the address you need.

Tel: 08457-741741
Minicom: 0131-244 1829
Fax: 0131-244 8240
Email: ceu@scotland.gov.uk
Website: www.scotland.gov.uk

Sport England
3rd Floor
Victoria House
Bloomsbury Square
London WC1B 4SE
Tel: 08458-508 508
Fax: 020-7383 5740
Email: info@sportengland.org
Website: www.sportengland.org

sportscotland
Caledonia House
South Gyle
Edinburgh EH12 9DQ
Tel: 0131-317 7200
Fax: 0131-317 7202
Email: library@sportscotland.org.uk
Website: www.sportscotland.org.uk

Sports Council for Northern Ireland
House of Sport
Upper Malone Road
Belfast BT9 5LA
Tel: 028-9038 1222
Fax: 028-9068 2757
Email: info@sportni.net
Website: www.sportni.net

Sports Council for Wales
Sophia Gardens
Cardiff CF11 9SW
Tel: 029-2030 0500
Fax: 029-2030 0600
Email: scw@scw.co.uk
Website: www.sports-council-wales.co.uk

SPRITO
24–32 Stephenson Way
London NW1 2HD
Tel: 020-7388 7755
Fax: 020-7388 9733
Email: the.nto@sprito.org.uk
Website: www.sprito.org.uk

The Stationery Office
PO Box 29
St Crispins
Duke Street
Norwich NR3 1GN
Tel: 0870-600 5522
Fax: 0870-600 5533
Email: customer.services@tso.co.uk
Website: www.tso.co.uk

UK Sport
40 Bernard Street
London WC1N 1ST
Tel: 020-7211 5100
Fax: 020-7211 5246
Email: info@uksport.gov.uk
Website: www.uksport.gov.uk

Appendix A

Terminology Associated with Sports Equity

Term	Definition
Disadvantage	As a result of discrimination (see definition below), some groups are deprived of all or some resources.
Discrimination	The action people take on the basis of their prejudices. Discrimination occurs when a prejudiced person has the power to put their prejudices into action, which results in unfair and unjust treatment. **Direct discrimination** occurs when someone is treated worse than other people in the same or similar situation. **Indirect discrimination** occurs when there is a rule or condition that applies to everybody, but people from a certain group are not able to meet it and there is no justifiable reason for having that rule.
Empowerment	Providing people with the knowledge, information and skills to enable them to have more control over decisions that affect their lives.
Ethnic group	Distinct groups identifiable by a combination of factors, including race, common nationality, traits, customs, culture and traditions[1].
Ethnic minority	An ethnic group within a society or region that is smaller in numbers than the majority population. A minority population is often a subordinate group of people, whose group members have significantly less control or power over their lives than members of a dominant or majority group[2].
Gender equality	Equal status, rights and responsibility for men and women.
Institutional racism	*The Macpherson Report*[3] defines institutional racism as: *The collective failure of an organisation to provide an appropriate and professional service to people because of their colour, culture or ethnic origin. It can be seen or detected in processes, attitudes and behaviour which amount to discrimination through unwitting prejudice, ignorance, thoughtlessness and racist stereotyping which disadvantage minority ethnic people.* This definition can be applied to all disadvantaged groups who are discriminated against.

1 and 2 Definition from *Clean Bowl Racism: A Report on Racial Equality in Cricket.* Reproduced with the kind permission of the ECB Racism Study Group.

3 Macpherson, W (1999) ***The Stephen Lawrence inquiry: report of an inquiry by Sir William Macpherson of Cluny***. London, The Stationery Office. Cm 4262-I

Term	Definition
Positive action	Enables employers and organisations to afford and encourage access to facilities, services, training or employment opportunities. For example, a national governing body may feel that a particular group of people is under-represented among its registered coaches. It decides to train more coaches and ensures that coaches from the under-represented groups are included in their plans[1].
Positive discrimination	Arises when a disadvantaged individual or group is singled out and treated more favourably than others. Positive discrimination is illegal. For example, a national governing body may feel that a particular group of people is under-represented among its registered coaches. Positive discrimination would occur if the national governing body proceeded to appoint people from this group without considering others, who were better qualified.
Prejudice	Describes negative feelings, thoughts and attitudes people have about other people that have no rational basis. Often ill-considered or pre-conceived and show bias towards certain groups of people. Everyone has prejudices about all kinds of things (eg food, clothes).
Racial discrimination	There are three main types of unlawful racial discrimination[2]: • **Direct discrimination:** when someone is treated worse on racial grounds than other people in the same or similar situation. • **Indirect discrimination:** when there is a rule or condition that applies to everybody, but people from a certain racial group are not able to meet it and there is no justifiable reason for having that rule. • **Victimisation:** when someone may be targeted for making a complaint under the Race Relations Act 1976.
Race	A group of individuals within a biological species. Groups of humans with distinct physical characteristics, such as skin colour and physical features[3].
Racial equality	Equal status, rights and responsibility for people of different racial groups.
Stereotyping	Grouping or labelling people because they share a particular trait(s), which is regarded as characteristic of that group. Stereotyping is usually negative and is frequently used to justify discrimination.

1 Based on a definition from *Tackling Racism in Your Sport* (Novlette Rennie, 24/25 November 1999).

2 Commission for Racial Equality (1998) ***Racial discrimination is against the law – campaign to increase young people's awareness of their rights under the Race Relations Act.*** Campaigns Pack. London, Commission for Racial Equality.

3 Definition from *Clean Bowl Racism: A Report on Racial Equality in Cricket.* Reproduced with the kind permission of the ECB Racism Study Group.

Appendix B

Organisations and Equity Initiatives

The Government has recognised the value of sport in promoting the inclusion of all groups of people in society and being used as part of programmes to reduce crime and anti-social behaviour. The Government agenda in relation to equity in society in general also applies to sport. As a result, many initiatives and organisations have been introduced to improve the sporting opportunities available to the key target groups. This appendix provides a summary of the key organisations and initiatives you should be aware of. It is divided into the following three sections:

- *Government Agenda* takes a look at key government initiatives designed to provide better sporting opportunities for disabled people, people from ethnic minorities and women and girls.
- *Sport Agenda* examines the progress made by key UK sports organisations.
- *Coaching Agenda* looks at coaching-specific initiatives.

This appendix will help you look beyond the *bigger picture* of government policy and understand why sports equity in coaching is so important.

Government Agenda

A Sporting Future for All (2000)

In April 2000, the Government launched a new sports strategy entitled *A Sporting Future for All.* This strategy seeks to give a lead in creating a more coordinated approach to improving sporting opportunities for all sections of the community and improving performance in international competitions. More specifically, it aims to improve the opportunities for disabled people, people from ethnic minorities and girls and women to participate, lead, coach and officiate.

Coaches have a central role to play in *A Sporting Future for All.* The strategy aims to ensure that coaches of sufficient quality and quantity are available from the grass roots of sport to the international arena.

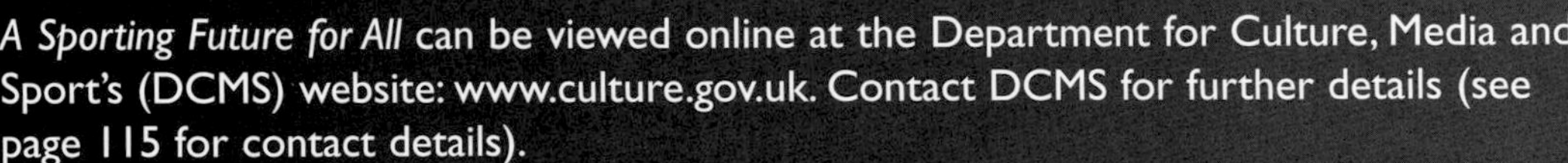

A Sporting Future for All can be viewed online at the Department for Culture, Media and Sport's (DCMS) website: www.culture.gov.uk. Contact DCMS for further details (see page 115 for contact details).

Policy Action Team 10 (PAT 10): A Report to the Social Exclusion Unit (1999)

Policy Action Team 10 (PAT 10): A Report to the Social Exclusion Unit recommends that sport be used as part of programmes to reduce crime and anti-social behaviour. It also highlights the need for an increase in the number of people from disadvantaged groups taking part in sport. This can only happen if sport is seen by these groups to be equitable and available to them.

PAT 10: A Report to the Social Exclusion Unit can be viewed online at the Department for Culture, Media and Sport's (DCMS) website: www.culture.gov.uk. Contact DCMS for further details (see page 115 for contact details).

Social Inclusion – Opening the Door to a Better Scotland (1999)

This report, published by the Scottish Office in 1999, highlights the potential role of sport in promoting social inclusion. The Scottish Executive's aim is to increase participation in sport by people at all age and ability levels, and to encourage young people to remain active in sport as they enter and progress through adulthood. Through **sport**scotland, the Scottish Executive will encourage improved access to sport by promoting equality of opportunity, whether the inequality is linked to poverty, geographical isolation, race or gender discrimination or disability.

Social Inclusion – Opening the Door to a Better Scotland can be viewed online at The Scottish Executive's website: www.scotland.gov.uk. Contact the Scottish Executive for further details (see page 116 for contact details).

The Macpherson Report (1999)

This is the report of the Stephen Lawrence Inquiry. The report found that institutional racism played a part in the flawed investigation by the Metropolitan Police Service of the murder of Stephen Lawrence. The Macpherson Report defines institutional racism as:

> *... the collective failure of an organisation to provide an appropriate and professional service to people because of their colour, culture or ethnic origin. It can be seen or detected in processes, attitudes and behaviour which amount to discrimination through unwitting prejudice, ignorance, thoughtlessness and racist stereotyping which disadvantage minority ethnic people.*
>
> *The Macpherson Report (1999)*[1]

As a result of the Macpherson Report and recommendations made by the Commission for Racial Equality, the Race Relations (Amendment) Act 2000 was introduced to extend the Race Relations Act 1976 to a wide range of public authorities (see page 80 for further information).

Copies of the Macpherson Report are available from The Stationery Office (see page 117 for contact details).

1 Macpherson, W (1999) *The Stephen Lawrence inquiry: report of an inquiry by Sir William Macpherson of Cluny*. London, The Stationery Office. Cm 4262-I

The Brighton Declaration (1994)

The first international conference on women and sport took place in Brighton in 1994. Aimed at decision-makers from governmental and non-governmental sectors, it focused entirely on women and sport. There were three main outcomes from the conference:

- An International Strategy on Women and Sport
- The Brighton Declaration
- The creation of the International Working Group on Women and Sport (IWG).

The Brighton Declaration is addressed to all governments and organisations that are responsible for, or have some influence over, women in sport. It complements all other laws, charters, codes and rules relating to women and/or sport and provides a comprehensive set of principles for the development of opportunities for women and sport. Its overriding aim is:

... to develop a sporting culture that enables and values the full involvement of women in every aspect of sport.

Women and sport and the challenge of change (Sport England, 1994)

The Brighton Declaration can be viewed online at the IWG's website: www.iwg-gti.org.

Sport Agenda

Sport England

16 Upper Woburn Place
London
WC1H 0QP
Tel: 020-7273 1500
Fax: 020-7383 5740
E-mail: info@sportengland.org
Website: www.sportengland.org

Sport England recognises that inequalities in sport exist and is working to change the culture and structure of sport to ensure that it becomes equally accessible to all. The Active Schools, Active Sports and Active Communities programmes are backed by support programmes for education and training, ensuring opportunity in sport, monitoring and evaluation. In addition, Sport England will be establishing measurable sports equity targets in all of its programmes to ensure that the following groups do not miss out:

- Girls and young women
- Black, Asian and other ethnic minority communities
- Disabled people
- People from deprived communities.

For nearly ten years, Sport England has promoted the principle of sports equity and worked with a wide range of governing bodies to develop equity policies. To accelerate progress in this area, Sport England has reviewed its policy aims to reflect a need to combat social exclusion, sustain cultural diversity and promote community development.

Sport England now has a formal Funding Agreement with the Department for Culture, Media and Sport (DCMS), which provides explicit and challenging statements of the outputs and levels of performance that Sport England is expected to deliver in return for the funding it receives from the DCMS.

All governing bodies are expected to produce equity policies and plans. Proposals should include how they intend to address issues such as equal opportunities in employment and greater representation of minority groups in formal positions within the organisation.

Sport England can provide the following support:

- Running Sport workshops:
  - A Club for All – Welcoming All Members of the Community
  - Sports Equity
- Sport-specific equity workshops
- Development seminars
- Equity guidelines and resources
- Expert advice.

sportscotland

Caledonia House, South Gyle
Edinburgh EH12 9DQ
Scotland
Tel: 0131-317 7200
Fax: 0131-317 7202
Email: library@sportscotland.org.uk
Website: www.sportscotland.org.uk

One of the main objectives of **sport**scotland's *Corporate Plan* is to increase participation in sport, particularly by those currently excluded. **sport**scotland has identified the need to work with:

- partners to increase participation by:
  - women
  - people with disabilities
  - people from minority ethnic groups
  - children and young people
- social inclusion partnerships to establish and implement a sports component.

In 2000, key research in the following three areas was undertaken for **sport**scotland:

- The role of sport in regenerating deprived areas
- Sport for people with disabilities
- Sport for minority ethnic groups.

The Role of Sport in Regenerating Deprived Urban Areas

This research report can be viewed online at the Scottish Executive Central Research Unit website: www.Scotland.gov.uk/cru.

Sport and People with a Disability: Aiming at Social Inclusion Summary and Sport and Minority Ethnic Communities: Aiming at Social Inclusion Summary

These research reports can be viewed online at **sport**scotland's website: www.sportscotland.org.uk. Copies are also available from **sport**scotland.

The recommendations from these research documents will provide the basis for all future work.

Football is not only one of the most popular participation sports in Scotland, it is also the fastest growing sport in popularity among young Scottish girls. **sport**scotland aims to give all girls and women the opportunity to develop their potential in the sport and is committed to working in partnership with the Scottish Football Association and local authorities to develop girls'/women's football.

sportscotland is also working closely with Scottish Disability Sport (see page 131) to maximise sporting opportunities for people with a disability.

Sports Council for Northern Ireland

House of Sport
Upper Malone Road
Belfast BT9 5LA
Tel: 028-9038 1222
Fax: 028-9068 2757
Email: info@sportscouncil-ni.org.uk
Website: www.sportni.org

The Sports Council for Northern Ireland (SCNI) is committed to providing equality of opportunity for everyone who wishes to participate in sport to the level of their choice and with due regard to the need to promote equality of opportunity between:

- persons of different religious belief, political opinion, racial background, age, marital status or sexual orientation
- men and women generally
- persons with a disability and persons without
- persons with dependants and persons without.

In working towards achieving this objective, SCNI has:

- adopted a *Sport in the Community Policy* document which moves SCNI to an anti-sectarian stance in an attempt to address issues of sectarianism, which impact on sport in Northern Ireland, through specific programmes and measures
- encouraged all national governing bodies with responsibility for developing sport for people with disabilities to amalgamate into one organisation – Disability Sports Northern Ireland (see page 130 for further details)
- supported initiatives such as the *Millennium Women's Sports Festival* (a joint Ladies Gaelic Athletics Association and women's soccer initiative) through a £30,000 Millennium Lottery enabling coaching and participation initiatives for young women interested in both sports to take place.

SCNI will continue to examine ways of increasing opportunities for people who are marginalised in society to access opportunities to take part in sport to the level of their choice. It has already started to review its current policies to ensure equality of opportunity for all, in accordance with Section 75 of the Northern Ireland Act 1998 (see page 85 for further details).

Sports Council for Wales

Sophia Gardens
Cardiff CF11 9SW
Tel: 029-2030 0500
Fax: 029-2030 0600
Email: scw@scw.co.uk
Website: www.sports-council-wales.co.uk

The Sports Council for Wales works to ensure that all people and all communities have access to sport. Priority is given to:

- young people
- women and girls
- people with disabilities
- people from ethnic minorities
- economically and recreationally disadvantaged groups.

An internal working group for women and girls was established in 1995. An action plan has been developed and is continually updated to ensure that sport-specific opportunities are made more equitable for girls. All governing bodies are encouraged to increase women's participation, coaching and officiating roles. A wider Women and Girls in Sport Advisory forum is also currently being established to advise the Sports Council for Wales on how it can improve its own programmes and influence its partners and the existing infrastructure of sport to respond to the needs of women and girls.

Recently, the Sports Council for Wales has established a small task force to examine the issue of social inclusion to identify ways in which SPORTLOT funds (fund set up to distribute the proceeds for sport in Wales from the National Lottery) can be invested in areas of economic and social deprivation not currently benefiting from SPORTLOT. The purpose of the Social Inclusion in Sport Challenge (SISC) is to find new ways of improving access to existing opportunities. The emphasis therefore is on increasing access, as opposed to developing new capital facilities. SISC will also seek to stimulate and develop projects, which have not been able to progress through normal funding mechanisms.

UK Sport

40 Bernard Street
London WC1N 1ST
Tel: 020-7841 9500
Fax: 020-7841 8850
Email: info@uksport.gov.uk
Website: www.uksport.gov.uk

UK Sport is leading on the development of an ethical framework for sport in the UK. A mechanism for coordination and consultation has been developed through the recently formed UK Coordinating Group on Ethics (UKCGE). This group currently includes representatives from all the home country sports councils and proposes to extend membership to include representation from **sports coach UK** and the British Olympic Committee.

UKCGE's Vision

The sports councils are committed to encouraging the highest ethical standards in sport in all parts of the UK. To achieve this, the sports councils will encourage everyone involved in sport to conduct themselves with integrity, transparency and accountability.

UKCGE meets quarterly and is charged with establishing a set of consistent and concise standards and values within sport, through the creation of an ethical framework. Special interest focus groups (eg women in sport, athletes with disabilities) meet on a regular basis to discuss specific issues.

UKCGE's Agenda of Ethical Issues for Sport

- Protection of the individual
- Corporate governance
- Anti-doping and other illegal practices
- Sporting conduct
- **Equity – this includes the prevention of discriminatory action against an individual on grounds of sex, age, race, religious beliefs, disability, political beliefs or marital and dependent status.**

Disability

Disability Sport Cymru
National Sports Centre for Wales
Sophia Gardens
Cardiff CF11 9SW
Tel: 029-2030 0500
Fax: 029-2030 0600
Email: scw@scw.co.uk
Website: www.disability-sport-cymru.co.uk

Disability Sport Cymru embraces two new schemes:

- National Performance Scheme
- Local Development Scheme.

The schemes aim to increase participation amongst disabled people and improve opportunities for talented disabled competitors to fulfil their potential. They are managed by two national officers coordinated by the Federation of Sports Associations for the Disabled (FSAD) and the Sports Council for Wales.

Disability Sports Northern Ireland (NI)
Unit 10
Ormeau Business Park
8 Cromac Avenue
Belfast BT7 2JA
Tel: 028-9050 8255
Textphone: 028-9050 8254
Fax: 028-9050 8256
Email: email@dsni.co.uk
Website: www.dsni.co.uk

Disability Sports Northern Ireland (Disability Sports NI) is the national umbrella body responsible for the coordination, promotion and development of sport for disabled people throughout Northern Ireland. It has initiated and organised a range of projects and works closely with sports providers and governing bodies of sport to promote the inclusion of people with disabilities in mainstream sport.

English Federation of Disability Sport (EFDS)
Manchester Metropolitan University
Alsager Campus
Hassall Road
Alsager
Stoke-on-Trent ST7 2HL
Tel: 0161-247 5294
Minicom: 0161-247 5644
Fax: 0161-247 6895
Email: federation@efds.co.uk
Website: www.efds.net

The English Federation of Disability Sport (EFDS) is the principal national agency responsible for the coordination and development of sport for disabled people in England. Launched in 1998, EFDS operates on a national and regional basis, and has the direct support and involvement of all major disability sports organisations. The EFDS four year national plan *Building a Fairer Sporting Society* gives greater detail on how EFDS works closely with the seven national disability sport organisations, national governing bodies of sport, local authorities and other statutory and voluntary organisations.

Scottish Disability Sport
Caledonia House
South Gyle
Edinburgh EH12 9DQ
Tel: 0131-317 1130
Fax: 0131-317 1075
Email: ssadsds2@aol.com
Website: www.scottishdisabilitysport.com

Scottish Disability Sport (formerly the Scottish Sports Association for Disabled People (SSAD)) was formed in 1962 to provide facilities for, and to encourage the development of, sport and physical recreation for disabled people. Scottish Disability Sport has now acted as the governing and coordinating body of all sports for all people with a disability for over thirty years.

Race

Sporting Equals

Commision for Racial Equality
Lancaster House (3rd Floor)
67 Newhall Street
Birmingham B3 1NA
Email: sportequal@cre.gov.uk
Website: www.cre.gov.uk

Sporting Equals is a national sports development initiative working to promote racial equality in sport throughout England. Established in 1998, the project is funded by Sport England in partnership with the Commission for Racial Equality.

Major initiatives launched by Sporting Equals include:

- *Racial Equality Charter for Sport* – a public pledge signed by the leaders of sport committing them to use their influence to create a world of sport in which all people can participate in watching, playing and managing sport without facing racial discrimination of any kind.
- *Achieving Racial Equality – A Standard for Sport* – a standard developed by Sporting Equals in partnership with the Commission for Racial Equality and Sport England to help sports organisations and national governing bodies (NGBs) plan, develop, evaluate and achieve racial equality in all aspects of sport. Organisations working towards the Standard are likely to have signed up to the *Racial Equality Charter for Sport* (see above). The Standard covers three main areas:
  - Commitment, policy and planning
  - Participation and public image
  - Administration and management.

There are three levels of achievement – preliminary, intermediate and advanced. Organisations are required to submit evidence of achievement in the three main areas at each level. Sporting Equals and Sport England verify the evidence and award organisations that achieve all the objectives at each level.

Tackle Racism in Rugby League campaign

The *Tackle Racism in Rugby League* campaign is a joint venture from the Commission for Racial Equality and the Rugby Football League. Launched in August 1996, the campaign aims to make rugby league clubs take positive action to eradicate all racist abuse from their grounds and to develop the game among ethnic minority communities in the clubs' local areas.

For more information about the *Tackle Racism in Rugby League* campaign, contact the British Amateur Rugby League Association (see page 114 for contact details).

Let's Kick Racism Out Of Football Campaign

During the 1993–94 football season, the Commission for Racial Equality and Professional Footballers Association (PFA) came together to launch the *Let's Kick Racism Out of Football* campaign. The campaign built on work which had already been begun by some supporters groups and individual clubs. The aim of the campaign was to send out a clear message that people from every background should be able to enjoy the game without fear of racist abuse, discrimination or harassment.

In 1997, Kick It Out was established as an independent organisation with funding from the PFA, The Football Association (FA), The Football Trust and the FA Premier League. The group took up the role of furthering the objectives of highlighting and campaigning against racism in football at all levels.

For further information about the *Let's Kick Racism Out Of Football* campaign, contact Kick It Out (see page 114 for contact details).

Women and Girls

Women's Sports Foundation (WSF)
3rd Floor, Victoria House
Bloomsbury Square
London WC1B 4SE
Tel: 020-7273 1740
Fax: 020-7273 1981
Email: info@wsf.u-net.com
Website: www.wsf.org.uk

The Women's Sports Foundation (WSF) is the only organisation in the UK that is solely committed to promoting and improving opportunities in sport, for women and girls, at every level. In 1999, WSF and Sport England launched a *National Action Plan for Women's and Girls' Sport and Physical Activity* to help organisations achieve gender equity in sport and physical activity. It aims to create a positive environment in which women and girls from different cultural, social and religious backgrounds have an equal opportunity and adequate resources to be involved in an activity of their choice at their chosen level and capacity.

For further information about the *National Action Plan for Women's and Girls' Sport and Physical Activity*, contact the WSF at the above address.

Coaching Agenda

sports coach UK
114 Cardigan Road
Headingley
Leeds S6 3BJ
Tel: 0113-274 4802
Fax: 0113-274 5019
Email: coaching@sportscoachuk.org
Website: www.sportscoachuk.org

sports coach UK is the only organisation in the UK that is dedicated to the development of coaching and coaches. **sports coach UK** believes that the composition of the coaching community should reflect that of the broader community in terms of gender, ethnic origin and ability. However, it recognises and acknowledges that disabled people, people from ethnic minorities and women and girls are under-represented in all spheres of coaching, umpiring and officiating.

sports coach UK*'s* equity action plan outlines the way in which the organisation intends to take positive action to increase the involvement of under-represented groups within the coaching community. It is currently implementing the plan in partnership with:

- Active Sports
- English Federation of Disability Sport
- local authorities
- national governing bodies
- Sport England
- Sporting Equals
- Women's Sports Foundation.

sports coach UK was one of the first organisations to be awarded the *Achieving Racial Equality – A Standard for Sport* at preliminary level (see page 132 for further details).

For further information about **sports coach UK's** equity action plan, contact the Equity Policy Development Team at the above address.

UK Vision for Coaching

Coaches have a major role to play in ensuring that sport is equitable. This role has been acknowledged in the *UK Vision for Coaching* published by UK Sport in 2000. The *UK Vision for Coaching* was developed to provide direction for coaches and coaching into the 21st century and has been endorsed by:

- British Olympic Association
- National Training Organisation for Sport, Recreation and Allied Occupations (SPRITO)
- Sport England
- **sports coach UK**
- **sport**scotland
- Sports Council for Northern Ireland
- Sports Council for Wales
- UK Sport.

The main objectives of the *UK Vision for Coaching* are set out in the panel below:

By 2012 the practice of coaching in the UK will be elevated to a profession acknowledged as central to the development of sport and the fulfilment of individual potential.

Coaching will have:

- professional and ethical values and inclusive and equitable practice
- agreed national standards of competence as a benchmark at all levels
- a regulated and licensed structure
- recognition, value and appropriate funding and reward
- a culture and structure of innovation, constant renewal and continuous professional development.

National Governing Bodies of Sport

Several national governing bodies of sport have taken the positive step of developing equity policies, which aim to include disadvantaged individuals or groups. The following are examples of good practice.

One 2 One Ability Counts: Football Opportunities for Disabled People

Organisations involved

- English Federation of Disability Sport
- Football Association
- One 2 One (financial support)

Main objectives

- Increase the number and expertise of coaches working with disabled footballers.
- Increase the number of disabled people participating in football in England at an appropriate level to them.

Examples of successful initiatives

- *Coaching Disabled Footballers* – developed specifically for the One 2 One Ability Counts programme, this course targets football coaches who are coaching disabled footballers and have, or are working towards, a football qualification. To date, 220 coaches have attended the course and 30 Football League and Premier League clubs offer coaching opportunities for disabled footballers.
- *Everton FC* – coaches have developed an exciting programme of football opportunities for disabled people on Merseyside. Regular coaching sessions for young disabled players have been established and coaches from the club's community programme have been providing coaching expertise in special schools and colleges. The club is now in the process of establishing a disabled section to provide regular training and competitive opportunities for disabled footballers of all ages.

Squash Rackets Association Coach Mentoring Pilot Scheme

Organisations involved

- Women's Sports Foundation (WSF)
- Squash Rackets Association (SRA)
- **sports coach UK**

Aims

- Train ten coach mentors.
- Enable eight women per county to become county coaches.
- Support women coaches to move into elite level coaching.

Black and Ethnic Minority Sport in Yorkshire (BEM Sport)

BEM Sport has been working in partnership with **sports coach UK** to develop more opportunities for representatives from black and ethnic communities to develop as coaches. The project is unique in that it has identified 20 local BEM people who will act as facilitators for the scheme. The facilitators have undergone initial generic coach development training and have been asked to do an audit of their local community and identify five people each interested in becoming new or better coaches. Each coach will then undergo further education and training supported by **sports coach UK** and national governing bodies.

Once training has been completed and these coaches have gained national governing body qualifications, the plan is to deploy these coaches back into their local communities to deliver quality coaching programmes. It is anticipated that some of these coaches and the young people they work with will then have better access to national programmes such as Active Sports.

Appendix C

Religious Festivals

It may not be appropriate for people to take part in sport during important religious festivals. The table below lists the main festivals celebrated by people from different religions. You should always take these into account when scheduling coaching sessions, events or competitions. The dates of the festivals may vary from year to year, so you are advised to consult the *Shap Calendar of Religious Festivals*[1] for details of dates in particular years.

The list is by no means exhaustive, so remember to consult with individual participants too.

Name of Festival	Religion	Description
Christmas Day	Christian	A major festival in the Christian faith, which celebrates the birth of Jesus, who Christians believe to be the son of God. Gifts are reminders of the offerings brought to the infant Jesus.
Easter Day	Christian	The most important festival of the Christian year when Christians celebrate the resurrection of Jesus. Easter eggs are given, which symbolise new life.
Eid-ul Fitr	Muslim	A three-day festival of the breaking of the fast, which comes at the end of Ramadan and at the start of the first of Shawwal, the tenth month of the Muslim calendar. It is a time for almsgiving, new clothes, good food, presents for children, family get-togethers and contact with friends. The community assembles for Eid prayer at the mosque or another suitable venue.
Hanamatsuri	Japanese and Buddhist	A flower festival marking the Japanese celebration of the Buddha Shakyamuni's birthday. The flowers accentuate the tradition that the Buddha was born in a garden, so floral shrines are made and an image of the infant Buddha is set in it and bathed.
Navaratri/Durga Puja/Dusserah	Hindu	One of the few festivals celebrated across India. Navaratri means *nine nights,* which is how long the festival lasts. The final three days are the most important.

1 Available from the Shap Working Party on World Religions in Education (see page 114 for contact details).

Name of Festival	Religion	Description
Passover/Pesach	Jewish	A major eight-day festival when Jews commemorate the Exodus from their slavery in Egypt. A highlight is the Seder meal held in each family's home at the beginning of the festival, when the story of their deliverance is recounted. Matzah (unleavened bread) is eaten throughout the festival, as are other foods that contain no leaven.
Ramadan	Muslim	The month of fasting from dawn to sunset. To the Muslim, fasting means abstaining from all food, drink, smoking and marital relations during daylight hours. It is an exercise in self-discipline and enables everyone to have some experience of deprivation. The fast is traditionally broken each evening by taking dates and water. Children may be encouraged to fast, although the full fast is not compulsory until maturity.
Yom Kippur	Jewish	The final day of the ten days of repentance. It is the holiest day of the year in the Jewish calendar. The Bible calls it the *Sabbath of Sabbaths* and it is marked by *afflicting the soul* – expressed through a total fast lasting 25 hours. Jews spend most of the eve and most of the day in prayer.

New Year Festivals

Some of the New Year festivals celebrated by people from different religions are listed below:

- Al-Hijra (Muslim)
- Chaitra (Hindu)
- Divali/Deepavali (Hindu)
- Ethiopian New Year's Day (Rastafarian)
- Ganjitsu (Japanese)
- Rosh Hashana (Jewish)
- Vaisakhi (Baisakhi) (Sikh)
- Yuan Tan (Chinese).

This list is not exhaustive, so remember to consult with individual participants too.

The text in this appendix is based on information from the ***Shap Calendar of Religious Festivals.*** *Reproduced with the kind permission of the Shap Working Party on World Religions in Education (**see page 114 for contact details**).*

Appendix D

Useful Suggestions for Working with Disabled People

Most people want to treat disabled employees, job applicants and customers the same way as everyone else but aren't always sure how to go about it. These suggestions aren't part of the Disability Discrimination Act 1995, but they may be useful when you meet disabled people.

Remember!

- Disabled people are individuals just like everybody else. Don't make assumptions about their abilities or their needs. Don't forget some impairments are hidden (eg epilepsy and mental illness).
- If you aren't sure how something might affect a disabled person, ask them for advice.

Communication

- If a disabled person is with someone, talk to the disabled person directly, not to the person who is with them. This also applies to a deaf person accompanied by a sign language interpreter.
- When talking to a deaf person, find out (if necessary, in writing) whether they lip-read. If they do:
  - make sure your face is in the light
  - look directly at the person
  - speak clearly and naturally
  - remember to keep your hands away from your face.
- When you first meet a blind person, introduce yourself. When you are going to move away, tell them. Don't leave them talking to an empty space.
- When you are talking to someone with a speech impairment, concentrate on what is being said, be patient and don't try to guess what they want to say. If you don't understand, don't pretend you do.
- If someone has difficulty understanding you (perhaps because they have a learning disability), be patient and be prepared to explain something more than once. Concentrate on using simple language.
- When talking to a wheelchair user, try to ensure that your eyes are at the same level as theirs, perhaps by sitting down. Don't lean on the wheelchair – it is part of the user's personal space.
- Avoid asking personal questions about a person's impairment, such as 'Were you born like that?' But an employer could ask 'Does your disability affect your ability to do this job?'
- If someone looks *different*, avoid staring. Concentrate on what they are saying, not on the way they look.
- If you are talking to an adult, treat them like an adult.

Assistance

- If someone looks as if they need assistance, offer it, but wait for them to accept before you help.
- When guiding a blind person, do not push or pull them. Ask if they would like to take hold of your arm. If there are any steps, tell them whether the steps go up or down.
- Remember that guide dogs for blind people, hearing dogs for deaf people and other assistance dogs, are working dogs, not pets. They should not be fed, patted or distracted when they are working.
- Above all, put yourself in the disabled person's place. Most of the above points are just good manners.

Language

Some of the words and phrases we use offend disabled people, because they suggest that the disabled person is dependent or helpless. Some words such as *cripple* or *retarded* have become terms of abuse or are used to make fun of disabled people. Below are some common words to avoid with suggested alternatives:

- Do not say ***the disabled***, use ***disabled people*** or ***people with disabilities***.
- Do not say ***suffering from, crippled by, afflicted by*** or ***a victim of***, use ***a person who has*** or ***a person with***.
- Do not say ***deaf and dumb***, use ***deaf without speech.***
- Do not say ***an epileptic***, use ***a person with epilepsy.***
- Do not say ***spastic***, use ***a person with cerebral palsy***.
- Do not say ***mentally handicapped*** or ***subnormal***, use ***a person with a learning disability.***
- Do not say ***confined to a wheelchair*** or ***wheelchair bound***, use ***wheelchair user.***

The text above and on pages 141 and 142 is based on information from DL200 (guidelines issued on behalf of the Minister for Disabled People. Prepared in conjunction with the National Disability Council and RADAR.). Reproduced with the kind permission of RADAR.

Coaching People with Learning Disabilities

- Be patient, tolerant, consistent and tactful, but ensure that participants understand the boundaries of acceptable behaviour.
- Break down complex skills into smaller steps.
- Establish the level to which instructions and directions are understood.
- Avoid using abstract models.
- Enable simple decision-making.
- Avoid drills that rely heavily on numeracy and literacy skills.
- Coach by showing and copying, not telling.
- Be aware that the motor skills and physical fitness of some participants may be generally poor due to lack of opportunities to participate in sporting activities or even take regular day-to-day exercise.

Appendix E

Glossary of Racial Terms

African	A native inhabitant of the continent of Africa. A person of African descent or ancestry. Africans are generally divided into North Africans (north of the Sahara desert) and South Africans (south of the Sahara desert). South Africans are generally, but not always, very dark skinned compared to the lighter skinned Northern Africans.
Asian	A native inhabitant of the continent of Asia. A person of Asian descent or ancestry. Asians are generally divided into South Asians, who are mainly of Indian origin, and Orientals, who are mainly of Chinese and Japanese origin. South Asians are generally, but not always, dark skinned.
Black-British	In its widest sense, a non-white citizen of Great Britain, including Asians and Orientals. Also used to describe non-white/non-English British inhabitants, who were born in Britain. In its narrowest sense, refers to British-born British citizens of African or Caribbean descent.
British-born African	A person of African descent or ancestry born in Great Britain.
British-born Asian	A person of Asian descent or ancestry born in Great Britain.
British-born Black	Non-white, British-born British citizens. In its narrowest sense, refers to British-born British citizens of African or Caribbean descent.
British-born Caribbean	A person of Caribbean descent or ancestry born in Great Britain.
Caribbean	A native inhabitant of the Caribbean. The majority population of the Caribbean is dark skinned, made up of peoples of African, South Indian, and oriental ancestry. Caucasians (white) person are prevalent.
Country of Birth	The actual country where an individual was born. Country of birth is distinct from nationality or ethnicity.
Country of Origin	The birthplace of a person and/or parents, and in some instances, grandparents.

Culture	The customary beliefs, social forms and material traits of racial, ethnic, religious, or social groups. Socially patterned human thought and behaviour. Culture is social heritage or tradition that is passed on to future generations. It is shared, learned human behaviour, a way of life.
Customs	Habitual course of action; usual behaviour; particular established way of behaving.
Ethnic	Relates to races or large groups of people classed according to common nationality, traits, customs, culture, and traditions. Ethnicity is more likely to denote origin of birth than political nationality.
Ethnic Groups	Distinct groups identifiable by a combination of factors, including race, common nationality, traits, customs, culture and traditions.
Ethnic Minority	An ethnic group within a society or region that is smaller in numbers than the majority population. A minority population is often a subordinate group of people whose group members have significantly less control or power over their lives than members of a dominant or majority group.
Ethnic Origin	One's parentage and ancestry, racial and geographical.
Ethnicity	Ethnicity has to do with group identification. When we talk of ethnicity, we indicate that groups and identities have developed in mutual contact rather than in isolation.
Mixed race/bi-racial	The offspring of a union between persons of different races.
Multi-cultural	Reflecting more than one cultural group; diverse cultures.
Plural society	A form of society embracing many majority groups and cultural traditions.
Race	A group of individuals within a biological species. Groups of humans with distinct physical characteristics, such as skin colour and physical features.
Race Relations	Inter-racial/ethnic connections usually for the promotion and maintenance of mutual interest, involvement, and benefits of all the groups concerned.
Racial	Concerning groups of individuals identifiable or differentiated by race.

Racialism	Discriminatory actions resulting from racist beliefs.
Racism	Conduct, words or practices, which advantage or disadvantage people because of their colour, culture, or ethic origin.
Racist	One who believes that populations should be categorised based on physical genetic features; that some races or ethnic groups are superior to others; that *inferior* groups should not have the same basic human rights as their superiors.
South Asian	A native inhabitant or descendent of southern Asia, including India, Pakistan, Bangladesh, and Sri Lanka. South Asians are generally, but not always, dark skinned.
Tradition	An inherited, established, or customary pattern of thought or action. Beliefs and customs handed down, generally by word of mouth, or by behaviour.
West Indian	A native inhabitant of the one of the Caribbean islands, which were formerly British colonies, known as the *West Indian* islands, together with British Guyana and British Honduras. The majority population of the (former) West Indian islands is dark skinned, made up of peoples of African, South Indian and oriental ancestry. Caucasians (white) persons are prevalent in most of the islands.
White English	The indigenous population of England (and Wales).
White Race	White skinned or light skinned race of people. Most often Europeans. The White race is also known as *Caucasian*.
White-Other	The minority white population in England, usually not English born, or second generation whites.

Definitions from ***Clean Bowl Racism: A Report on Racial Equality in Cricket.*** *Reproduced with the kind permission of the ECB Racism Study Group.*

Appendix F

Levels of Participation for Disabled Participants

The model in Figure 1 will help you understand the opportunities available to disabled participants.

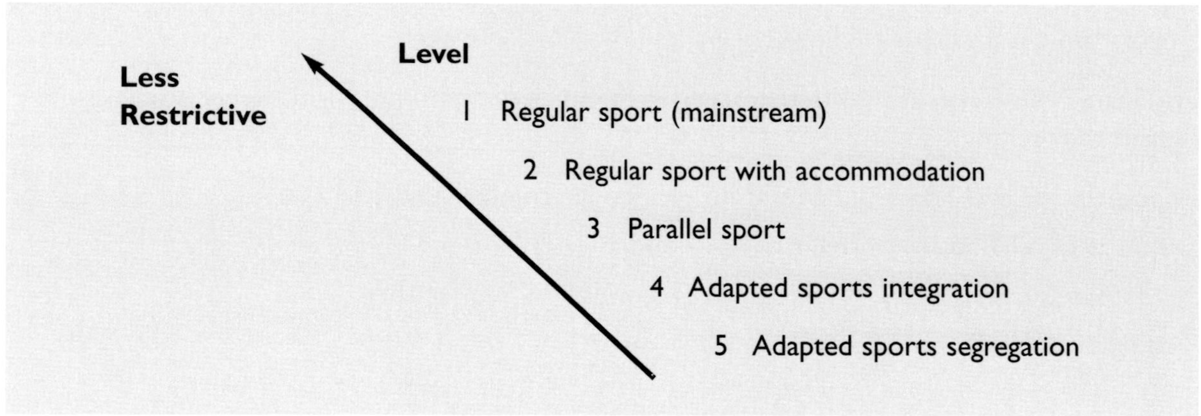

Figure 1: The Winnick Model
Adapted from Winnick, PJ (1987) An Integration Continuum for Sports Participation Adapted Physical Activity Quarterly, Vol 4 (3) 158

This model was developed by Winnick in 1987 to show the different levels at which disabled participants could train and compete.

Level 1: regular sport (mainstream)

Total integration (coaching, competition and social) of disabled participants into mainstream competition and clubs (eg an athlete with a learning disability training, competing and socialising in a local athletics club).

Level 2: regular sport with accommodation

Integration of disabled participants into regular competition, clubs and coaching with some flexibility in the rules and regulations to enable integration and equal opportunities to non-disabled peers (eg wheelchair tennis players and non-disabled tennis players playing up and down doubles where wheelchair players are allowed two bounces of the ball).

Level 3: parallel sport

Disabled participants competing in the same event as their non-disabled peers but in their own section (eg wheelchair athletes in a marathon).

Level 4: adapted sports integration

Disabled and non-disabled participants taking part in an adapted sport, in a segregated setting (eg forming teams for the purposes of developing a wheelchair basketball competition).

Level 5: adapted sports segregation

Disabled participants competing in a competition solely for that particular disability group (eg goalball[1]).

Disabled participants can be accommodated at various levels of the Winnick continuum depending on factors such as:

- individual choice
- level of ability
- type of sport
- opportunities available to the participant.

Participants could also be at different levels in Winnick's continuum for different purposes. For example they might:

- compete at Level 1 locally but aim for elite competition at Level 5
- train at Level 1 but compete at Levels 3 and 5
- compete at Levels 1 or 2 in one sport, or Levels 3 or 5 in another
- compete at Level 5 and coach at Levels 1 and 5.

Segregation, Integration and Inclusion

To what extent should disabled participants be ***integrated*** into mainstream sport and when should they be ***segregated***? This is a difficult question because you need to weigh up a number of issues such as the:

- type of sport – some sports are readily accessible and individual, so integration is relatively easy (eg archery, swimming)
- views of the disabled participant – some prefer to train and compete only with other disabled participants, others prefer to be fully integrated
- views of the coach – his/her ability and willingness to adapt and organise sessions appropriately to facilitate integration
- views of other participants – they may feel they are not getting sufficient attention or their training needs are not being fully met, if programmes have been adapted to allow disabled participants to be fully integrated
- views of others – such as parents and helpers who may question the appropriateness of integrating a disabled participant into the session.

1 Goalball is an indoor ball game which is played by visually impaired people on a tactile court using a ball with a bell in it.

Appendix G

Participant's Questionnaire

On reflection in the last month, did your coach:

• give you attention?	not at all	hardly ever	occasionally	often	a great deal
• give you an opportunity to make your own decision?	not at all	hardly ever	occasionally	often	a great deal
• establish a good climate in training?	not at all	hardly ever	occasionally	often	a great deal
• spend time discussing goals and priorities?	not at all	hardly ever	occasionally	often	a great deal
• encourage you to take responsibility for yourself?	not at all	hardly ever	occasionally	often	a great deal
• positively receive your ideas and act on them?	not at all	hardly ever	occasionally	often	a great deal
• take an interest in your life outside sport?	not at all	hardly ever	occasionally	often	a great deal

On reflection, in the last month how often did you feel:

• like giving up your sport?	not at all	hardly ever	occasionally	often	a great deal
• disenchanted with training/your sport?	not at all	hardly ever	occasionally	often	a great deal
• valued by the coach?	not at all	hardly ever	occasionally	often	a great deal
• highly committed to your training and sport?	not at all	hardly ever	occasionally	often	a great deal

Appendix H

Action Plan Templates

This appendix contains a blank copy of the action plans used in Activity 8 (pages 98 to 100) for you to photocopy and use as and when required.

SHORT-TERM IMPROVEMENTS/CHANGES

What?	How?	When?
1		
2		
3		

LONG-TERM IMPROVEMENTS/CHANGES

	What?	How?	When?
1			
2			
3			